SUCCESS WITH
HERBS

SUCCESS WITH
HERBS

Yvonne Cuthbertson

GUILD OF MASTER CRAFTSMAN
PUBLICATIONS LTD

For Anna and Richard

First published 2006 by
Guild of Master Craftsman Publications Ltd
166 High Street, Lewes, East Sussex, BN7 1XU

Text © Yvonne Cuthbertson 2006
© in the Work GMC Publications Ltd

Illustrations by Penny Brown
Photographs © Yvonne Cuthbertson

ISBN 1 86108 412 9

British Cataloguing in Publication Data
A catalogue record of this book is available from the British Library

A catalogue record of this book is available from the British Library

Production Manager: Hilary MacCallum
Managing Editor: Gerrie Purcell
Editor: Alison Howard
Managing Art Editor: Gilda Pacitti
Designer: Andy Harrison

Set in Futura

Colour origination by Altaimage
Printed by and bound by Sino Publishing, China

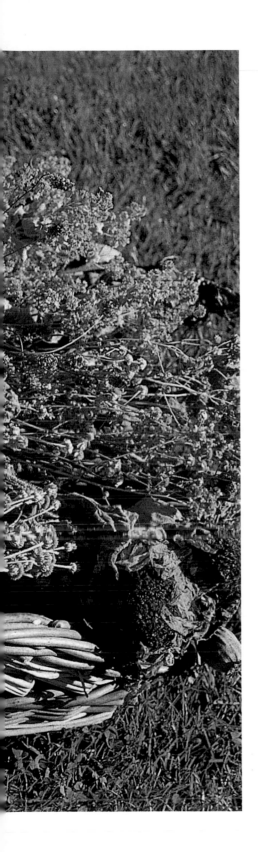

Contents

LEFT **Dried herbs displayed in a basket**

Introduction

Herb gardening is rather like embarking on a journey into the past; a nostalgic trip evocative of all the charm and delights of a more leisurely age. Perhaps its greatest joy is that it is easy, inexpensive and satisfying, and combines all the pleasures of the flower garden with the usefulness of the vegetable plot. A little effort is soon rewarded by a treasury of shape, colour, texture, and taste. Herbs are accommodating plants and if they are given the right conditions, they will reward you with vigorous, healthy growth, luxuriant foliage and rich, aromatic perfumes. They are now generally accepted as valuable garden plants in their own right, and can make stunning displays as well as being functional.

Herbs have held their place in our gardens for centuries. They are attractive, romantic and timeless, and reminiscent of bygone days when our ancestors cultivated them not only for their usefulness, but also for the aura of 'magic' that surrounded them. Herb gardens have a certain domestic quality, providing unity to the planting by giving it shape and purpose. Their aesthetic appeal and decorative and ornamental qualities are as important today as they have always been, and each plant has its characteristic scent, foliage, texture and shape.

Herb gardens are pleasant places in which to walk, especially on a hot summer day when their aromatic scents permeate the whole garden. There is also something very satisfying about stepping outside your kitchen door and picking a handful of fragrant herbs. Herb gardens allow plenty of scope for the imagination, and herbs adapt to a number of styles and designs. Planning and planting them is fun. It prompts you to look at gardening books and catalogues, to visit nurseries, garden centres, herb gardens and even museums and libraries for research as you collect ideas and choose which herbs to grow. A decorative herb garden can give pleasure during every season if year-round interest is taken into account when planning. The wide range and variety of herbs on offer makes it easy to introduce them into any garden, whatever its size or design. Anyone can grow herbs, even if they live in an apartment. Many gardeners cultivate herbs in containers, which is an excellent idea if space is limited.

With today's ever-increasing interest in ecology, natural products and alternative medicines, herbs have once more come into their own. They are utilitarian and practical, and they are also easy to include in any garden layout, allowing the gardener to find plants that are suitable for every situation. Herbs are ideal for making a garden that is unique, individual, and reflects the personal tastes of its creator.

Yvonne Cuthbertson, 2006

LEFT **This large container has a massed planting of assorted herbs**

What is a herb?

Herbs are amenity plants that have been used from very early times to provide food and flavouring, medicine and perfumes. The word herb is derived from the Latin *herba*, meaning *grass*, and herbs have been grown throughout the ages for the benefit of both humans and animals. Before the advent of industrialization and advancements in science and technology, all plants were considered important to mankind. Nowadays, most people tend to be less involved with nature and the process of actually growing food. As a result, we now have a limited concept of the potential and possible uses for herbs, and we generally relegate them to the kitchen to be used for flavouring food or adding as garnishes.

ABOVE **Feverfew produces masses of daisy-like flowers**

12

ABOVE **Goldenrod has upright stems and pointed leaves, and its yellow flowers are borne in late summer**

Many plants that we now regard simply as garden flowers were once classified as 'useful' and, accordingly, were highly-prized as herbs. Chrysanthemums and wallflowers, for example, were traditionally grown for their medicinal properties, while roses were widely used both in medicines and cosmetics. Nasturtiums, poppies, geraniums and sunflowers all qualified as herbs, again because of their usefulness. Ox-eye daisies were much sought after by herbalists,

WARNING:
Never ingest or use herbs without taking advice from an appropriate authority. Some herbs or parts of herbs are poisonous, and some can cause allergic reactions.

ABOVE **Nasturtiums make an excellent garnish for salads, giving them both colour and flavour**

and marigolds – not to be confused with French marigolds, which should not be eaten – were used by cooks as a pot herb. Goldenrod achieved fame as a 'wound' herb because of its healing properties.

Accordingly, in the main section of this book and in the A–Z Directory that follows, you will find some plants that are nowadays popularly regarded simply as garden flowers. They have been included because in the past they have been considered valuable for culinary, aromatic, medicinal or cosmetic reasons. These qualities have given them the status of herbs.

ABOVE **Cowslips are one of the best herbs for attracting bees into the garden during spring**

13

CHAPTER 1

Where to grow herbs outdoors

Herbs are a striking and invaluable feature of any garden, and a surprisingly large selection can be grown in a small amount of space. They are also extremely adaptable and easy to cultivate. Herbs can be planted in a variety of situations; the vegetable plot, the rockery and the herbaceous border, to name but a few. And yet, there is something extremely satisfying about having a separate, attractively designed herb garden: the impact of combined scents, shapes, textures and colours can be quite stunning.

SIZE AND LOCATION

A herb garden can range from the smallest practical measurement, 6ft (1.8m) by 4ft (1.2m) to 25ft (7.6m) by 18ft (5.5m) or larger. This depends on the space available, your chosen

ABOVE **A traditional American herb garden at the American Museum in Bath, England**

SHELTER

Herbs dislike wind, so a sheltered spot is important. This can be achieved simply and effectively by planting hedges of herbs such as English lavender *Lavandula angustifolia*, rosemary, hyssop *Hyssopus officinalis*, or traditional box *Buxus sempervirens*, all of which will tolerate clipping. Alternatively, trellises with roses or honeysuckle trained up them will help. If you are able to site your garden within a walled area or behind a fence, so much the better. The garden could be 'walled in' with banks of earth which can afterwards be planted with pennyroyal *Mentha pulegium* or Roman chamomile *Chamaemelum nobile*.

LEFT **Most herbs, including hyssop, need sun to thrive**

ABOVE **Honeysuckle can be trained around pillars**

design, the herbs you wish to grow, and the time available for maintenance, although herbs are relatively maintenance free. Do not be over-ambitious; start small, growing the herbs you will use and then add to them later on.

Before you can plan your herb garden, you need to establish its location. Many herbs originated in Mediterranean countries and prefer plenty of sun, some exceptions being the mints *mentha*, chervil *Anthriscus cerefolium*, bergamot *Monarda didyma* and angelica *Angelica archangelica*. The ideal position for a herb garden, therefore, is in a south- and/or west-facing part of the garden that slopes slightly towards the sun.

Always plant your herbs in the conditions they prefer. Make sure that you have easy access: firm, all-weather paths are essential. Remember also that some herbs are very fussy about soil and position, while others are extremely adaptable. For instance, rosemary *Rosmarinus officinalis* will grow almost anywhere, although it will not flourish in cold winters.

ABOVE **Box is a hardy ornamental plant, here grown in a pot but widely used as formal hedging**

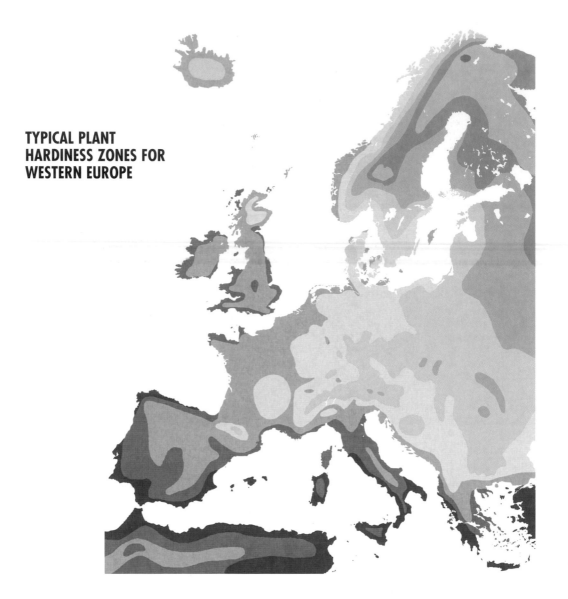

**TYPICAL PLANT
HARDINESS ZONES FOR
WESTERN EUROPE**

GROWING HERBS ACROSS THE WORLD

Herbs can be grown in many parts of the world. Conditions in some parts of Europe are similar to those found in Britain, so the same herbs should grow happily. In other areas, such as around the Mediterranean, adjustments may be needed, such as extra watering or planting in shady areas. Factors such as extremes of cold and hours of sunlight must also be taken into account.

Across North America, there are more extreme variations of temperature than those found across Britain and Northern Europe. To grow herbs successfully the factors that will need to be taken into consideration include the hours of cold weather in winter, how hot the summers are, and whether the climate is damp or dry. The charts on these pages should help you to determine your chances of success.

16

**TYPICAL PLANT
HARDINESS ZONES
FOR NORTH AMERICA**

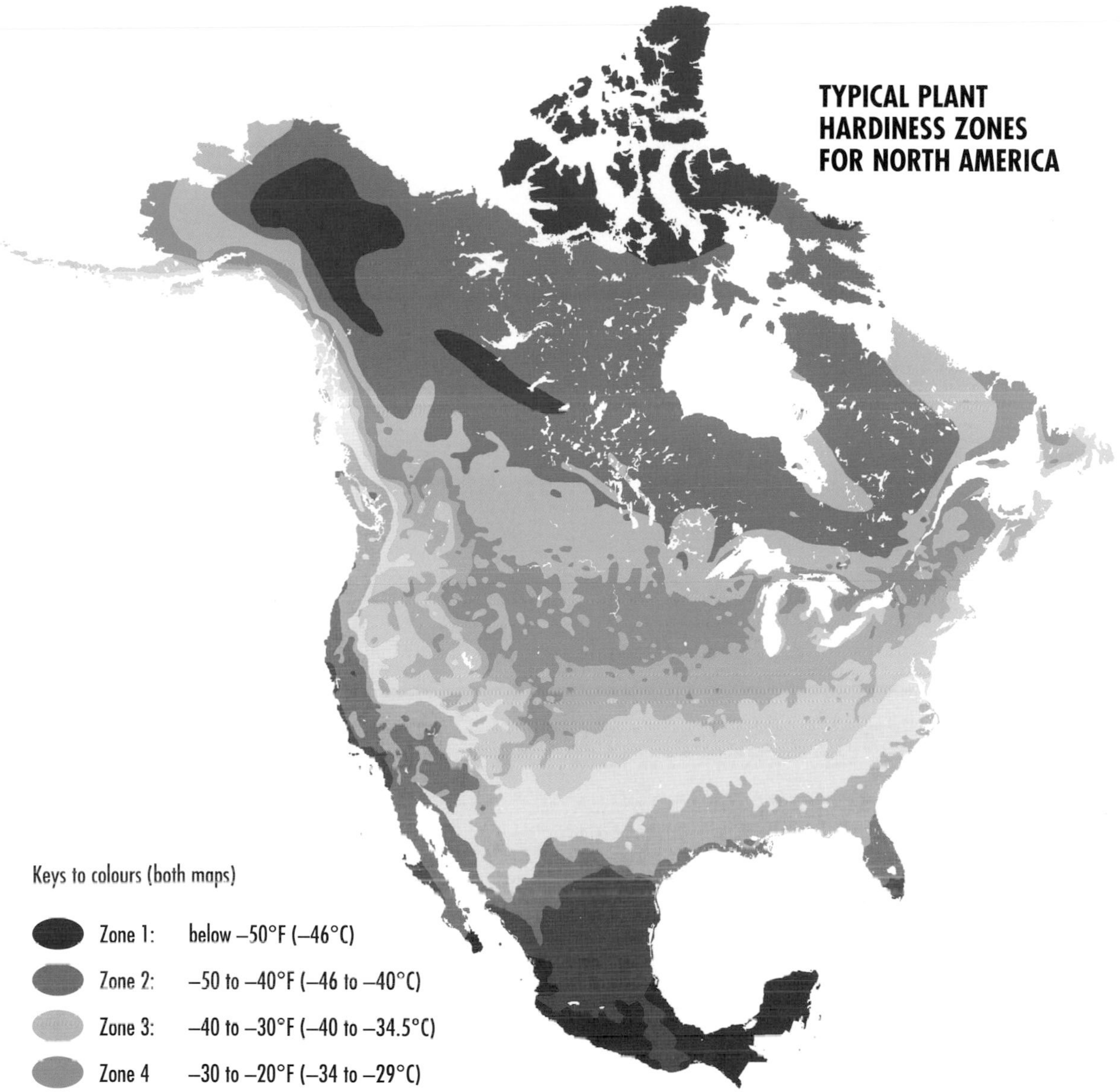

Keys to colours (both maps)

- Zone 1: below −50°F (−46°C)
- Zone 2: −50 to −40°F (−46 to −40°C)
- Zone 3: −40 to −30°F (−40 to −34.5°C)
- Zone 4: −30 to −20°F (−34 to −29°C)
- Zone 5: −20 to −10°F (−29 to −23°C)
- Zone 6: −10 to 0°F (−23 to −18°C)
- Zone 7: 0 to 10°F (−18 to −12°C)
- Zone 8: 10 to 20°F (−12 to −7°C)
- Zone 9: 20 to 30°F (−7 to −1°C)
- Zone 10: 30 to 40°F (−1 to 4°C)
- Zone 11: above 40°F (above 4°C)

HOW TO USE THESE MAPS

Each entry in the plant directory lists the relevant zones where it should be possible to grow the plant successfully, based on these heat-zone maps. Find your location on the map, and you can then identify the zone that your area belongs to. Do not forget to take into account that cities are warmer than rural locations. Planting shelter belts of trees, or planting against a sunny, south-facing wall and/or in raised, well-drained beds, can help to give plants better conditions in which to thrive.

17

TYPES OF SOIL

The acidity or alkalinity of soil depends on how much calcium it contains: too little and the soil is acid, too much and it is alkaline. These levels are measured by the pH scale which reads from 0–14. Soils with a pH above 7 are alkaline, those with a pH below 7 are acid. The pH of most soil is somewhere between pH6 and pH 7.5 making it more or less neutral, and most herbs will tolerate these kinds of conditions. A pH reading of 7 is ideal.

You can determine the pH level of your soil by buying a pH testing kit and following the simple instructions. It will indicate the approximate pH value, which is usually adequate as all plants possess some tolerance.

ACID SOIL

Not many plants thrive in acid soil. The pH of slightly acid soil can be raised by digging lime into your plot during preparation. The best limes

ABOVE **Horseradish will thrive in clay soil**

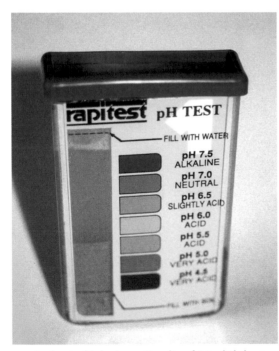

ABOVE **A soil testing kit showing a pH reading of 6.5, which denotes a slightly acid soil**

to use are ground chalk or limestone, the finer the grade the better. Great care should be taken when you are using lime because it is caustic. Choose a day when no wind is blowing, and keep children and pets well away from the area. A mask can be worn if desired. Wear gloves when handling the lime, and avoid contact with the skin or the eyes. If this happens, wash it off immediately using cold water. If you have any cause for concern, seek medical advice immediately.

HEAVY CLAY SOIL

Soil that contains a lot of clay should be dug over in autumn and left exposed to winter frosts. Add large quantities of organic matter during late winter/early spring, because its fibrous nature will help open up the soil and, gradually, will cause smaller and smaller crumbs to form from the large clods of earth. Leaf mould and bark are excellent soil conditioners. Bark should be left on the surface to rot, then worked into the soil. Seaweed, spent hops and spent mushroom compost also work well. Plenty of organic matter such as this will need to be worked in, and should be added regularly every year. Adding grit or sand will alter the texture of the soil, but will do little to improve its basic structure.

On the plus side, clay is probably one of the richest soils as it holds on to plant foods and releases them slowly. Some herbs will thrive in clay soil, including comfrey, elecampane, horseradish, Jacob's ladder and tansy, but generally, plants will struggle in heavy clay soils. The ground easily becomes compacted because there are very few air spaces between the particles. If your soil is very heavy, you might like to consider growing your herbs in raised beds.

CONSTRUCTING A SOAKAWAY

Light, free-draining soil is usually low in nutrients and does not hold moisture. Mediterranean herbs thrive under such conditions, but others will not. Herbs such as mint will benefit if you add organic matter four to five weeks before planting to supply nutrients and helt the soil to retain moisture. Do not do this any earlier or it may be leached by the rain. Humus contains gel-like substances that bind soil particles together to form crumbs, and aid moisture retention.

Condition and quality of soil is important in every herb garden. Most herbs will thrive on relatively poor soil if it is not waterlogged. If your soil is always sodden after prolonged rain, you should improve its water-draining ability. This can often be achieved simply by forking in coarse sand at the rate of 4lb per square yard (2kg per m^2). If the drainage problem is severe, it can be solved by constructing a soakaway.

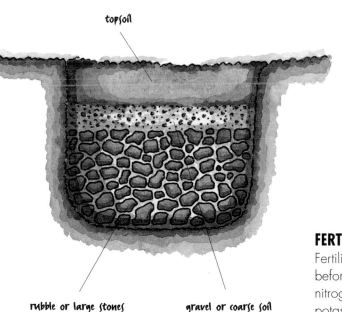

topsoil

rubble or large stones

gravel or coarse soil

1 Dig a hole at least 2ft (60cm) square, and 3ft (90cm) deep at the lowest point in the garden.

2 Fill to within 12in (30cm) of the top with rubble or large stones.

3 Cover with a 6in (15cm) layer of gravel or coarse sand.

4 Finish with a 6in (15cm) layer of topsoil to ground level.

FERTILIZERS

Fertilizer may be added to soil 10–12 days before planting. Compound fertilizers contain nitrogen to encourage leaf and stem growth, potash to aid flower and fruit formation, and phosphate which will boost the roots. Try to avoid using artificial fertilizers: the organic or herbal kind are the best.

ABOVE **Most ground needs a thorough digging to prepare it for a herb garden**

DIGGING YOUR PLOT

Before planting, dig your soil over thoroughly. Generally, soil only needs to be dug to one spade's depth. One exception to this rule is the land that surrounds a newly-built house, where the use of heavy machinery has compacted the topsoil. The builders may have placed a few inches of fresh soil over it to make it look good, but do not be fooled. The hard layer of compacted earth that is left below the surface soil will impede drainage and prevent plants from rooting. The only solution to this problem is double digging.

Dig your plot over in autumn. If you are single digging, throw the soil forward as you go so that you have a neat trench alongside you. Put organic matter on the slope of the soil that has been thrown forward, so that it will eventually become thoroughly mixed in through all levels of the soil. Refill the trenches with the amount of soil taken out to keep the digging level. In spring, turn the soil over thoroughly, removing all weeds and debris. Break it up with a spade or fork and then rake it until a fine tilth is obtained.

ABOVE **A herb bed with traditional box hedging, clipped to give the bed its customary uniformity**

PLANTING

- Keep to the planting distances recommended on the seed packets or plant labels.
- Harvest herbs regularly. Trim and keep them in check as necessary to control both height and spread and to keep your design neat and well-defined.
- Remember that herbs grow at different rates according to soil, position and the climate of the area in which you live. Some of them will also self-seed.
- The overall number of plants you use will depend upon the size of your design or construction.
- Note the season of interest of each herb.

ABOVE **A sunny herb garden**

PLANNING YOUR HERB GARDEN

Once you have decided on the size and site of your herb garden, plan it on paper so that you can be sure to blend the colours of foliage and flowers and the textures of leaves, and to avoid planting tall herbs in front of mound-forming varieties. Ask yourself what kind of design is suitable, what groups of plants you will grow, and if your garden will follow a theme or pattern. Draw to scale to make it easier to appreciate the size of the beds; to assess the proportions – height and spread – of the various herbs; and to compare the space between the beds with the dimensions of your plants. Measure carefully and make sure you position permanent features correctly. Do not forget to include existing features such as hedges, fences, walls, large trees and the house.

Think where to place paths: a herb garden will need them around its borders as well as between its beds. Ideally they should be wide enough to trundle a wheelbarrow along, and if necessary for wheelchair access. If your garden design is to be informal the paths could be curved, but make sure they lead somewhere, perhaps to a seat. Do not forget to place a focal point, which is traditional and which relieves the flatness: a bird bath, a sundial, or a potted bay tree are ideal. Ornaments must never dominate or ruin the impact of your design. It is easy to destroy the elegance of your herb garden, so choose wisely.

Use separate sheets of paper to work out planting schemes. These can be altered, if necessary, when you have tried out possible variations in your garden. All-round interest should be considered. Herb gardens can look bare in winter, so be sure to include some evergreens such as rosemary, bay, hyssop and rue as the backbone of your design, planting them throughout according to their height. Then think about the positioning of perennial herbs such as lemon balm, fennel, bergamot and lovage. Finally, choose the annual herbs which should be arranged according to their height, spread, the colour of flowers and foliage, and the texture of leaves. Within your chosen design, herbs can be planted informally and arranged so that, for example, culinary and pot pourri herbs are kept separate, or formally using large numbers of just a few species to create 'carpets' of herb bedding.

21

FORMAL DESIGNS

When you have chosen your site, think about the shape and size of your garden. Most herb gardens are rectangular. Whatever design you decide upon, remember that it must be practical. A lot of herb gardens are informal and semi-formal, although those that have the greatest impact are usually formal. Remember that many herbs do not grow to their 'prescribed' sizes, while some of them romp away, often to twice their normal size. This can result in one plant masking another as it jostles for space and light, so you will need to discover how various herbs will grow in your particular soil. It is also important to know what type of soil you have and to note down the season of interest of each of your chosen plants: some will start to grow early in the year, others much later, and they will also flower at different times. Bear in mind foliage, colour and texture: you may wish to grade them or you might prefer to spread them randomly throughout.

PLANTING SUGGESTIONS

Borage (*Borago officinalis*)
Chives (*Allium schoenoprasum*)
German chamomile (*Matricaria recutita*)
Golden marjoram (*Origanum vulgare* 'Aureum')
Lavenders (*lavandula*)
Apple mint (*Mentha suaveolens* 'Variegata')
Purple leaved sage (*Salvia officinalis* 'Purpurascens')
Caraway thyme (*Thymus herba-barona*)
Golden lemon thyme (*Thymus citriodorus* 'Aureus')

Note: plant one herb per square

YOU WILL NEED:

Paving slabs, number depending on the size of design
String
Short wooden stakes or pegs
Spirit level
Length of board
Piece of wood with a right-angle
Garden tools
Humus/organic matter
Selection of herbs

CREATING A CHESSBOARD GARDEN

A chessboard design uses paving slabs that are laid in an attractive square formation like a chessboard. Spaces of soil exactly the same size as the paving slabs are left between them, and used for planting the herbs.

1 Select the site and measure it, taking into account the number and size of the paving slabs you intend to use. Allow for possible breakages when you are buying slabs.

2 Draw your plan to scale, marking in the position of slabs, areas of soil, focal point and herb plantings.

3 Mark out the area of your plot using string and stakes/pegs.

4 Dig the soil, removing perennial weeds and large stones. Dig in humus/rich organic matter as you go.

5 Rake the soil to a fine tilth and level with the edge of the board.

6 Check that the corners are at right angles, using the wood with a right-angle. For a square garden, check that all sides are of equal length.

7 Lay the first slab in the top left-hand corner, using the string as a guide. Make sure that it rests snugly against the string. Check that it is level in all directions, using a spirit level. If not, add or remove a little soil underneath one corner. Miss out a space of earth equal in width to the slab and lay the next stone. Repeat along the length of the plot, again resting the final slab snugly against the string.

8 Start the second row by placing the first slab in front of the first area of soil in the completed row with the corners touching, again using the spirit level. Continue in this way until the total area has been completed, leaving you with a chessboard effect.

9 Remove the string and stakes/pegs. If you wish, lay a gravel path, add gravel around the edges, or plant a hedge around the edge using, for example, cotton lavender.

10 Plant the herbs. Water in well and keep watered until they are established.

BELOW **A completed chessboard garden**

The keynote of a knot garden was its uniformity, a result of the type of hedging plants chosen and the way in which they were clipped.

Ideas from knot gardens can be adapted and included in today's smaller garden. Knot gardens have the advantage that the herbs are within easy reach for harvesting and upkeep. Precision is vital, as is frequent maintenance so that the low hedges remain trim and the geometrical symmetry neat.

Thorough planning is vital for a successful knot garden. Determine the measurements of the site and draw the proposed design to scale on graph paper. This will allow you to visualize the size of the beds, to assess the proper placement of plants and to obtain a good, overall image of your planned knot.

LEFT **Geometric knot herb garden at the Red Lodge, Bristol, England**

CREATING A KNOT GARDEN

Some formal, geometric herb gardens take the form of a knot. First recorded in the fifteenth century, knot gardens were originally contained within a square or rectangular plot, with each knot pattern outlined precisely by low, clipped hedges of evergreen herbs, such as box, cotton lavender, hyssop and lavender. Designs were often taken from family crests, heraldic devices, or the entwined initials of the garden's owners.

YOU WILL NEED:
Measuring tape
Humus/organic matter
String
Short wooden stakes or pegs
Squeezable bottle of chalk dust
Piece of wood with a right-angle
Selection of herbs

ABOVE **Examples of knot garden designs**

1 Measure the site and draw your design on graph paper.

2 Dig the soil, removing all perennial weeds and large stones. Dig in humus/rich organic matter as you go.

3 Working from the plan, transfer the design to the plot. Measure out the design on the ground and mark it with the string and stakes/pegs. Fill in the details with the chalk powder. Check that the corners are accurate, using the wood with a right-angle. For a square garden, check that all sides are the same length.

4 Place the focal point – sundial, bird bath, or formal rose bush – in the centre.

5 Plant hedging herbs to define the knot at their correct planting distances. When they begin to spread, clip the tops and the sides that face the walks or beds, to encourage them to grow more quickly.

6 Lay the pathways and plant the beds with herbs. Plant evergreen and perennial herbs first, giving plenty of thought to their foliage and flower colour.

7 Water in well and keep watered until the herbs are established.

PLANTING SUGGESTIONS
Hedges
Box (*Buxus sempervirens*)
Cotton lavender (*Santolina chamaecyparissus*)
Lavenders (*lavandula*)
Rosemary (*Rosmarinus officinalis*)
Shrubby germander (*Teucrium fruticans*)
Winter savory (*Satureja montana*)

Tall herbs
Angelica (*Angelica archangelica*)
Elecampane (*Inula helenium*)
Fennel (*Foeniculum vulgare*)
Lovage (*Levisticum officinale*)
Mullein (*Verbascum thapsus*)

Centrepieces
Sundial, bird bath, statue, potted bay tree

Paths
Bricks, pebbles, gravel

Medium-sized herbs
Coriander (*Coriandrum sativum*)
Feverfew (*Tanacetum parthenium*)
Hyssop (*Hyssopus officinalis*)
Lemon balm (*Melissa officinalis*)
Mints (*mentha*)
Sages (*salvia*)
Sweet basil (*Ocimum basilicum*)
Tarragon (*Artemisia dracunculus*)

Short and edging herbs
Anise (*Pimpinella anisum*)
Basil thyme (*Acinos arvensis*)
Chives (*Allium schoenoprasum*)
Roman chamomile (*Chamaemelum nobile*)

LEFT **Hedging of box, lavender or rosemary is essential for knot gardens**

ABOVE **A herb wheel, about six weeks after planting**

CREATING A HERB CARTWHEEL

Another all-time favourite is a herb cartwheel. This uses an old cartwheel which is treated with preservative, painted on one side with exterior varnish or white exterior paint, and set lightly into the prepared soil. A variety of different herbs of similar heights and rates of growth can be planted between the spokes to create a quickly-made miniature herb garden.

As old wooden cartwheels are expensive and may be hard to find, a replica can be made using halved log rolls of manageable size. Take note of recommended planting distances when placing the plants, and divide them or transfer to another part of the garden if and when they outgrow the design, so that the cartwheel always looks neat and compact. Do not allow it to become overgrown, straggly, or untidy.

YOU WILL NEED

Log rolls, painted with preservative then
  painted or varnished with exterior varnish
  (the number needed will depend on their
  size and that of the planned herb wheel)
Eight lengths of prepared timber
  (to form the spokes of the wheel)
Flowerpot or bulb bowl, varnished or
  painted, for the wheel 'hub'
Short wooden stakes or pegs
String

PLANTING SUGGESTIONS

Chives: height 4–24in (10–60cm), spread
  12in (30cm). Use three plants.

Compact marjoram: height 6in (15cm),
  spread 12in (30cm). Use three plants.

Corsican mint: height 1–4in (2–10cm),
  spread indefinite. Use one plant.

Dwarf lavender: height 6–12in
  (15–30cm), spread 6–18in (15–45cm).
  Use two plants.

Golden lemon thyme: height 10–12in
  (25–30cm), spread 24in (60cm).
  Use one plant.

Marjoram 'White Anniversary': height
  6–10in (15–25cm), spread 6–8in
  (15–20cm). Use four plants.

Nasturtium: Height and spread 12in
  (30cm). Use three plants.

Parsley: Height 12–32in (30–80cm).
  Use three plants.

1 Mark out the area. Attach the string to one of
the stakes/pegs and plunge into the ground at the
centre of the proposed circle. Attach the second
peg to the end of the string, at the required radius.
Holding the string taut, mark out the circumference
of the circle on the ground.

2 Dig the soil, removing turf or gravel (if
necessary) and perennial weeds and large
stones. Dig in humus/rich organic matter as
you go. Remove some of the topsoil and place
on a sheet of polythene. Loosen the subsoil.

3 Place the bulb bowl or flowerpot at the centre of the circle. Place the spokes in the form of a cross to divide it into quarters. Tap into place.

4 Place two more spokes diagonally so that you have eight separate segments of equal size, and tap into position.

5 Position the edging logs and tap firmly with the mallet. Replace some of the excavated topsoil into each of these segments.

6 Plant the herbs, remembering to allow for growth and spread. Water in well and keep watered until established.

CREATING A HERB LADDER

An old wooden ladder is ideal for this design. Treat it with a preservative before use, and then stain the ladder or paint it on one side using exterior paint. Place it in position in prepared soil and plant your herbs between the rungs of the ladder. As an alternative, bricks can be used to achieve a similar effect. If you use this method, position the uprights of the 'ladder' first and fit the brick 'rungs' in afterwards.

PLANTING SUGGESTIONS

Chives: height 4–24in (10–60cm), spread 30cm (12in). Use two plants.

Double chamomile 'Flore Pleno'): height 6in (15cm), spread 18in (45cm). Use one plant.

Lemon thyme: height 10–12in (25–30cm), spread 24in (60cm). Use one plant.

Parsley: height 12–32in (30–80cm), spread 12in (30cm). Use three plants.

Pennyroyal: height 4–16in (10–40cm), spread indefinite. Use one plant.

Sweet marjoram: height 24in (60cm) spread 18in (45cm). Use one plant.

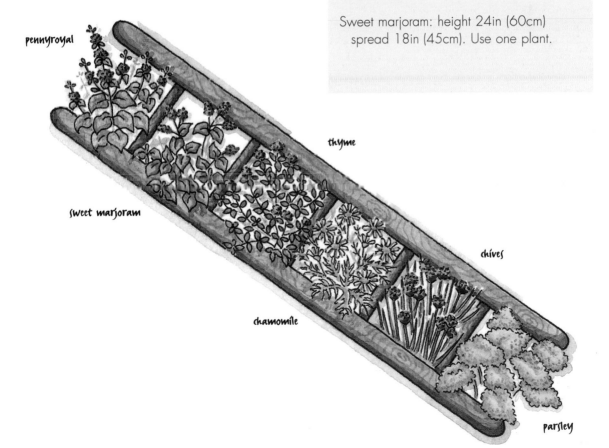

pennyroyal

thyme

sweet marjoram

chives

chamomile

parsley

SEMI-FORMAL DESIGNS:

Planted in a well-drained, sunny position, a border of mixed herbs will provide interest and colour to the garden. Those noted for their attractive foliage should be included, for example tansy and the sages, along with those with wonderful aromatic foliage such as rosemary and lavender.

CREATING A HERB BORDER

Herbs with taller habit should be planted towards the back – angelica, lovage and elecampane are a few examples – with the smaller plants to the front. The border can be edged with chives, parsley or thyme and backed by medium-sized herbs such as cotton lavender, marjoram, winter savory or sweet cicely. To avoid formal planting, herbs should be set out in groups of three or five – uneven numbers are best – and gaps filled with colourful annuals such as blue borage or red poppies.

The size of the garden shown in the example is 6ft (1.8m) long, giving six planting spaces of 15 x 12in (38 x 30cm).

KEY TO ILLUSTRATION:

1　Comfrey
2　Cotton lavender
3　Chives
4　Lovage
5　Golden marjoram
6　Trailing nasturtium
7　Dill
8　Cowslips
9　Parsley
10　Rue
11　Pot marigolds
12　Winter savory
13　Chamomile
14　Golden thyme
15　Elecampane
16　Borage
17　Sweet marjoram
18　Variegated lemon balm
19　Feverfew
20　Tansy
21　Golden marjoram
22　Trailing nasturtiums
23　Angelica
24　Sage
25　Sweet cicely
26　Mullein
27　Lavender
28　Poppies
29　Rosemary
30　Thyme 'Silver Posie'

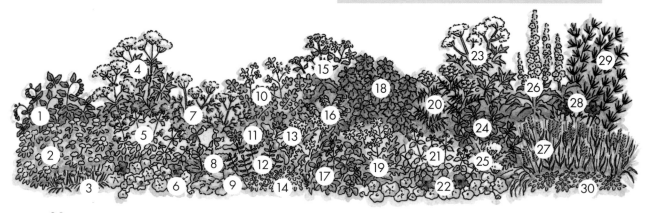

PLANTING SUGGESTIONS

Tall herbs

Angelica: height 6–8ft (1.8–2.5m), spread 18–43in (45cm—1.1m). Use one plant.

Elecampane: height 10ft (3m), spread 5ft (1.5m). Use one plant.

Fennel: height 6ft 6in (2m), spread 18in (45cm). Use one plant.

Lovage: height 6ft 6in (2m), spread 39in (1m). Use one plant.

Mullein: height 6ft 6in (2m), spread 39in (1m). Use two plants.

Rosemary: height and spread 6ft 6in (2m). Use one plant.

Medium-sized herbs

Cotton lavender: height 8–20in (20–50cm), spread 24in (60cm). Use three plants.

Curry plant: height 24in (60cm), spread 39in (1m). Use one plant.

Feverfew: height 24in (60cm), spread 18in (45cm). Use three plants.

Golden marjoram: height and spread 30in (75cm). Use three plants.

Hyssop: height 18–24in (45–60cm), spread 24–36in (60–90cm). Use one plant.

Lemon balm: height 12–32in (30–80cm), spread 12–18in (30–45cm). Use five plants.

Mints: height variable, spread indefinite. Use one plant.

Rue: height 24in (60cm), spread 18in (45cm). Use five plants.

Sages: height and spread variable, depending on species. Use three plants.

Sweet cicely: height 3–6ft 6in (1–2m), spread 2–4ft (60cm–1.2m). Use one plant.

Tarragon: height 18–39in (45cm–1m), spread 12–15in (30–38cm). Use three.

Winter savory: Height 4–16in (10–40cm), spread 3–8in (7–20cm). Use five plants.

Colourful annuals

Borage: height 12–39in (30cm–1m), spread 6–12in (15–30cm). Use three plants.
Poppies: height and spread variable, depending on species. Use three plants.

LEFT Lush growth in an informal corner herb bed

INFORMAL HERB GARDENS

Whether by accident or design, herb beds are usually informal because many herbs fail to know their proper limits. An informal garden can be beautiful as plants jostle for space and overflow on to pathways, but you should take care that your herbs do not get out of control. When planning an informal herb garden, follow your intuition rather than a regular plan or pattern as informal gardens tend to obscure boundaries. Planting should be close so that no soil is visible once the plants are established. Herbs that self-seed, for example borage, foxglove and evening primrose, will grow on in a random fashion. Plant in informal groupings.

ABOVE **Part of an informal herb garden, showing the interest, texture and form that herbs can provide**

Herbs may also be planted informally in beds with other ornamental plants. This is a useful ploy if you do not have enough space for a separate herb garden. A charming idea is to include herbs that will attract butterflies and bees, such as common or English lavender and pink carnation.

The example is a large herb bed 22ft long by 11ft wide (6.75 x 3.4m). It will need stepping stones placed randomly to give access to the herbs for harvesting and general maintenance.

LEFT **An informal, old-fashioned herb garden that illustrates the beauty of plants jostling for space and overflowing on to pathways**

KEY TO ILLUSTRATION:

1	Lovage	16	Marjoram
2	Angelica	17	Sage
3	Goldenrod	18	Pot marigold
4	Elecampane	19	Lemon balm
5	Mullein	20	Hyssop
6	Bronze fennel	21	Lavender
7	Southernwood	22	Scented leaf geranium
8	Curry plant	23	Thyme
9	Mint	24	Feverfew
10	St John's wort	25	Pinks
11	Marshmallow	26	Chives
12	Salad burnet	27	Pennyroyal
13	Poppies	28	Lily of the valley
14	Rue	29	Heartsease
15	Cumin	30	Chamomile

PLANTING SUGGESTIONS FOR A BACKDROP OF A WALL, TRELLIS OR HEDGE

Tall herbs

Angelica: height 3–8ft (1–2.5m), spread 18–43in (45cm–1.1m). Use one plant.

Bronze fennel: height 4–5ft (1.2–1.5m), spread 18in (45cm). Use one plant.

Elecampane: height 10ft (3m), spread 5ft (1.5m). Use one plant.

Foxglove: height 3–6ft 6in, (1–2m), 6ft 6in (2m) in 2nd year, spread 10in (25cm). Use five plants.

Goldenrod: height to 5ft (1.5m), spread 18–24in (45–60cm). Use three plants.

Lovage: height 6ft 6in (2m), spread 39in (1m). Use one plant.

Marsh mallow: height 39–47in (1–1.2m), spread 24–36in (60–90cm). Use one plant.

Mullein: Height 6ft 6in (2m), spread 39in (1m). Use three plants, unevenly grouped.

Medium-sized herbs

Curry plant: height 24in (60cm), spread 39in (1m). Use one plant.

English lavender: height and spread 24–36in (60–90cm). Use two plants.

Evening primrose: height 1–5ft (30cm–1.5m), spread 9–12in (22.5–30cm). Use five plants.

Feverfew: height 24in (60cm), spread 18in (45cm). Use three plants.

Hyssop: height 18–24in (45–60cm), spread 24–36in (60–90cm). Use three plants.

Lemon balm: height 12–32in (30–80cm), spread 12–18in (30–45cm). Use three.

Rue: height 24in (60cm), spread 18in (45cm). Use three plants.

Sage: height 24–32in (60–80cm), spread 39in (1m). Use one plant.

St John's wort: height 12–24in (30–60cm), spread 6–18in (15–45cm). Use five plants.

Salad burnet: height to 30in (75cm), spread 12in (30cm). Use five plants.

Southernwood: height 39in (1m), spread 12–24in (30–60cm). Use three plants.

Spearmint: height 12–39in (30cm–1m), spread indefinite. Use one plant.

Thyme: height 12–18in (30–45cm), spread 24in (60cm). Use two plants.

Wild marjoram: height and spread 18in (45cm). Use three plants.

Plants for infilling

Borage: height 12–39in (30cm–1m), spread 6–12in (15–30cm). Use five plants.

Field poppy: height 8–36in (20–90cm), spread 4–18in (10–45cm). Use five plants.

Pot marigold: height and spread 20–28in (50–70cm). Use two plants.

ABOVE **Herb beds positioned, dug and partly planted**

HERB GARDEN MAINTENANCE

Once established, you will find general upkeep and maintenance of your herb garden relatively easy. A weekly meander around, weeding, harvesting, clipping and dead-heading is usually sufficient. During the summer months, the occasional organic feed can be given. As a rule all but the moisture-loving herbs, such as sweet cicely, sorrel, mint, bergamot and comfrey, will tolerate dry conditions for short periods, but all herbs need to be watered occasionally, particularly angelica and parsley. A mulch such as chipped bark, cocoa shell, gravel or coarse grit will help to conserve water in the soil.

Herbs need regular dead heading of flowers, and dead and shrivelled leaves need to be nipped off to deter pests and diseases. Rotting vegetation also harbours pests and diseases, so remove it. It may also be necessary to give plants that need formal shaping several clips a year until you achieve the required shape. Cut back withered or broken branches to soil level to help strengthen the plant. Weeds are seldom a problem as herbs are rampant growers.

Annual herbs should be dug up at the end of the growing season. Perennials should be cut off at their base; stake them and write the name of each on a marker, placing it close to each plant, so that you will know what will come up the following year. Evergreens should also be cut back vigorously. For winter protection in colder area, apply a layer of straw to your herb garden, beds and borders.

35

CHAPTER 2

Growing herbs indoors

Herbs are not house plants, but many herbs can be kept indoors for a while without permanent harm. Most of the herbs that grow successfully in pots outside, and those that die down when summer has ended, will grow indoors for most of the year. Herbs grown indoors are not as long-lived and are more likely to become drawn and elongated. Remember that all herbs prefer to be outside in the summer.

When choosing herbs for indoor growing, be aware that glass can reduce light by 30–50 per cent. Many herbs fare better on a windowsill, though they will also grow well under fluorescent lights. If your plants become drawn and spindly, the chances are that they are not getting enough light. Sun-loving herbs need at least six hours of sun each day to flourish. Turn herbs each day for an even amount of sunlight on all sides.

Kitchens are not suitable for keeping herbs, as temperatures tend to fluctuate. Fumes from cooking, domestic gas and oil also take their toll on plants. Bathrooms make excellent growing rooms, as do conservatories, greenhouses and sunny porches.

ABOVE **A selection of herbs growing in pots on a well-lit windowsill**

HERBS FOR GROWING INDOORS

If you do not have space for a large herb plot, there is a way to increase the number of herbs you can grow. Many herbs will thrive quite happily indoors on a sunny windowsill.

SCENTED-LEAF GERANIUMS

These are ideal for the blind or partially sighted, and flourish indoors. The flowers of scented-leaf geraniums are fairly insignificant so they are mainly cultivated for their perfume, which is released when the leaves are brushed gently. Scented-leaf geraniums can grow to gigantic proportions if left untrained, so severe pruning is necessary. There are many species, with a vast choice of perfumes. They will not grow to the same height as they would in the garden, but will give great pleasure if they are re-potted in fresh compost every year and moved to a larger pot when necessary. *Pelargonium* x *citrosum* (*P. crispum* hybrid), *P. crispum* 'Variegatum' and 'Prince Rupert' geranium all have lemon-scented foliage, the latter with greyish leaves, 1in (2cm) wide, with crisped or curled edges. Peppermint-scented geranium is shrubby and sprawling, with particularly erect stems up to 39in (1m) in length. Its leaves are triangular and grow to 5in (12.5cm) across.

ABOVE **Scented-leaf geraniums will flourish indoors**

SAGES

These make excellent conservatory plants. Try growing pineapple sage *Salvia elegans* 'Scarlet Pineapple'), with its long, pointed leaves and bright scarlet flowers, 1½in (4cm) long. Common sage will also grow well indoors, as will 'Icterina', which has gold, variegated leaves; 'Purpurascens', which has dark purple leaves or 'Tricolor', which has irregularly-slashed, creamy-white foliage. Sages can be kept in any room, and should be clipped back to a manageable size and shape.

ABOVE **Sage 'Icterina' has golden, variegated leaves**
RIGHT **Purple sage will grow well in a conservatory**

ABOVE **Pot marigolds require a cool position**

POT MARIGOLD

The tiny-petalled, round, orange flower heads brighten up the dullest corner. Marigolds are in flower for most of the year if dead-headed regularly, but do not like heat. Pinch out the top shoot and, if you want a short, sturdy plant for container growing, make sure it gets plenty of sunlight and keep the soil moist.

THYME

Common or garden thyme is an attractive plant with small, round, grey-green aromatic leaves. It is a useful culinary herb, so it is ideal for keeping indoors so it can be cut regularly.

LEMON BALM

The deep-veined leaves of this plant have a strong lemon scent. It can be invasive in the garden, so it is ideal for a pot on a windowsill.

ROSEMARY

An ideal plant for the conservatory, it flourishes in a bright position, but needs a cooler temperature of around 15°C (60°F) to produce flowers. It rarely grows to more than 39in (1m) in a container.

PARSLEY

This can be grown in a variety of ways, including planting it in a small strawberry pot or a crocus pot, which has pockets set all over the surface, or in an indoor hanging basket.

ABOVE **Lemon balm, wild marjoram and lemon verbena growing on a sunny windowsill**

ABOVE **Sweet basil will grow well on a sunny windowsill**

LEMON VERBENA

Aloysia triphylla is a deciduous shrub with pointed, lemon-scented leaves and sprays of mauve flowers in summer. Grow it out of doors in a pot that is small enough to take indoors for winter. A conservatory is an ideal place, or the windowsill of a sun room. Do not be tempted to place it in a warm room as it will wilt rapidly and fail to thrive. Lemon verbena, like bay, prefers filtered sun and a rich soil.

BASIL

Ocimum basilicum 'Purple Ruffles' or 'Dark Opal' will grow happily indoors, usually to a height of 18–24in (45–60cm). Grow in a free-draining compost, and do not allow it to become waterlogged. Sweet basil and lemon-scented basil also grow well indoors.

BAY

Small specimens of sweet bay (*Laurus nobilis*) can be grown in pots and will also live quite happily on a windowsill indoors. They are best cultivated from cuttings taken in summer or bought as pot plants. Other herbs can be planted in the same container as bay; try thyme, winter savory or marjoram.

ABOVE **Bay is often grown in a pot for decoration**

ABOVE **Thyme, parsley and sage growing on a sunny windowsill**

ABOVE **Roses grown indoors must have plenty of light**

ABOVE **Myrtle is valuable for its foliage, flowers and fruits**

ROSES

Young scented roses, of standard or bush varieties, will also flourish indoors in pots. Prune in mid-winter by removing weak shoots and cutting back the other stems to just above the fourth strong bud above the base.

When you bring roses indoors, increase the temperature slowly from around 41°F (5°C) at night, to 46°F (8°C) by day in mid-winter, to about 55°F (13°C) at night and 64°F (18°C) by day in late spring. Place in a well-lit spot. Keep the compost moist and spray the foliage to maintain humidity. When buds start to form, feed with a liquid fertilizer every 7–10 days. Once the plants have stopped flowering move them out of doors. Try the hybrid tea 'Ena Harkness' with its red blooms, or the floribunda 'Fleur Cowles' with its pink, scented flowers.

ABOVE **Winter savory (*Satureja montana*) has whorls of white flowers, which appear in summer**

MYRTLE

Grown indoors, the height and spread of *Myrtus communis* can be confined to 2–3ft (60–90cm). The plant has aromatic foliage and lovely flowers followed, usually, by decorative fruits. It is ideal for growing in a cold conservatory.

MARJORAM

Sweet marjoram has greyish-green leaves and attractive creamy flowers and is a useful culinary herb. Pot marjoram also grows well in containers, though its flavour is not as good.

JASMINE

The fragrant *Jasminum polyanthum* bears scented, white flowers in early spring and can be trained around canes. It can be grown in a cool conservatory, but it is a vigorous grower that must be kept under control.

SAVORY

There are three types of savory, all of which are similar in flavour. Their strong, peppery flavour is excellent in stuffings and stews. Summer savory is an annual, so it is not suitable for growing indoors. Creeping winter savory has a spread of about 12in (30cm) and is best grown in a herb rockery. Winter savory is a small, woody perennial with thin, dark green, very aromatic leaves. It best used fresh as its leaves can be rather tough when they are dried. It is ideal for growing in a pot on a windowsill.

CURRY PLANT

This has attractive silver foliage with a stong pepper scent, and yellow button-like flowers. *Helichrysum italicum* can also be grown outdoors all year round. It is also a useful insect repellent.

PLANTING HERBS FOR GROWING INDOORS

When planting herbs indoors where there is central heating, remember that they will require plenty of fresh air and adequate watering. Herbs with large, soft leaves in active growth or in small pots will need frequent watering, but do not over-water. Root rot fungus will flourish in waterlogged soil and important air pockets in the soil can be eliminated. The occasional soak, though, is much appreciated.

All annuals should be started from seed and perennials from cuttings. Sow annual and biennial herb seed in late summer in 3in (7.5cm) pots to start them off. Bring them indoors, moving them on to larger pots as they grow.

Herbs can be grown from seed either by buying packets, or by harvesting your own. Annuals and biennials such as dill, borage, summer savory and chervil will give quick results, although others will be slow to raise. Sow seed indoors by sprinkling it on a tray of compost, following the instructions on the packet. Usually, the seed should be sown ¼–½in (6–12mm) deep. Use a suitable seed growing medium, and make sure that it is level and

slightly firmed. Water lightly and place the tray in a plastic freezer bag. Inflate the bag by blowing into it and tie the top, keeping the tray away from direct sunlight. When the seeds have germinated (time will vary according to the herb), remove the bag and when the seedlings are large enough to handle, transplant them into another pot or tray to give them more room.

If you only need a few specimens of each herb, plant the seed in pots. Sow thickly because clumps of seedlings are much easier to transplant. Do not let the seedlings get burned by strong sunlight, and once true leaves appear above the seed leaves, transplant clumps of five or six seedlings into small pots. Place on a windowsill to provide early pickings.

An easy way to raise herbs from seed is to buy special packs that contain seed for one species of herb and peat pots of compost designed to help germination. A transparent plastic dome is provided to cover the planted pots and act like a miniature greenhouse, so the seed soon begins to germinate. Herb seed is most at risk when it begins to germinate. If it dries out the seed will not germinate, and if too much water is applied to the seedlings before their roots develop, they will collapse and die. Try using a mist spray to keep the soil just moist. Thin out the seedlings when they appear and transfer the peat pot into a plant pot filled with compost. Leave the roots of the herbs to grow through the peat pots into the compost and continue growing to their full size.

Small pieces of the roots of herbs such as mint, as well as clumps of chives, can be lifted in late summer and planted up in pots. Mint can be left outside until after the first frost. Herbs such as tarragon and lemon balm should be lifted by mid-autumn, potted up and left to establish in a shady corner for about a month. As they need time to acclimatize before being brought indoors, leave them outside during the day at first, and bring them in at night.

ABOVE **Basil seedlings can be grown in a seed tray**

ABOVE **Mint can be potted up and taken indoors**

In late summer/early autumn, cut back herbs that are intended to be brought indoors to around 6in (15cm) high. Lift enough of the herb to fill a 4–6in (10–15cm) pot containing a multi-purpose compost. If you have the space available, it is a good idea to plant up three pots of any herb that you use frequently. In this way you will have one plant in use, a new one ready to use, and one recovering. Cut the first plant back to around 1in (2.5cm) in late summer or early autumn. Harvest the second plant for a month, then cut any remaining shoots back. Harvest the third plant for the following month and cut it back. By this time the first plant should be ready to use again.

FILLING A POT

The health and vigour of pot-grown herbs will depend largely on the rooting medium that you use. The best compost for pot plants is well aerated, holds moisture, is free-draining and contains plenty of nutrients.

METHOD

1 Place a layer of drainage material such as crocks at the bottom of the pot.

2 Add about 2in (5cm) of horticultural sand – to stop the compost from clogging – and then fill the pot two-thirds full with a soil-less compost.

3 Make a hole in the middle of the compost and set the herb into it, settling the compost around its roots.

4 Fill with compost to 1in (2.5cm) below the rim of the pot.

5 Water well with a fine spray to settle in the plant, then stand the pot in a saucer of gravel to allow the drainage of excess water and keep the atmosphere around the plant humid.

6 Feed with a liquid fertilizer at the intervals recommended by the manufacturer.

AFTERCARE

After planting, water very sparingly only when the compost seems to be drying out. Plants that are kept too wet are likely to rot. Herbs grow best in a temperature that does not drop below 60°F (15°C). They do not like sudden draughts or changes in temperature, but the room should be ventilated when the weather permits. Good light is also important, but use shading to prevent the foliage from burning if it is particularly sunny. Be vigilant regarding insect pests such as aphids and carrot fly. Newly-potted herbs will not require feeding for at least a month because of the nutrients already present in the new compost. Most herbs flourish better in groups; they are easier to water and they respond well to the mini-climate that grouping creates. Mist spray during summer to maintain good humidity.

THE POT-BOUND PLANT

It is important to recognize when a plant is pot bound. You will find that it is growing very slowly, even in good light and warmth with regular watering and feeding and good air circulation. The roots of the plant may be growing through the drainage holes of the pot. To make sure, remove the plant from its container. If the roots are thickly matted and twine around the pot, then your plant is ready to be potted-on.

POTTING-ON

Healthy plants soon outgrow their pots and need to be potted on regularly if they are to grow and keep their shape. Make sure that you move gradually up the pot sizes as placing a plant in a pot that is too big will encourage a weak root system and the plant will look out of proportion

ABOVE **A herb removed from its pot. Its roots are thickly matted, and it is ready to be potted-on**

with its pot. Round pots have a number that represents their diameter and their approximate height. Tap-rooted herbs such as borage, dill, chervil and parsley do best in deep pots. The new larger pot should allow at least 1in (2.5cm) of extra space around the plant that is to be potted on. Make sure the herb you are potting-on is moist.

1 Place drainage material such as crocks or gravel at the bottom of the pot, followed by a layer of compost.

2 Remove the herb by inverting the pot across your upturned hand with the plant between your fingers. Tap the rim against a hard surface to loosen the pot and lift it off the plant.

3 Tease out the roots of the herb and sit it on the compost.

4 Fill in the sides of the pot with more compost, firming it with your fingers. When finished, the rootball should be covered with about ½in (1cm) of compost.

5 Water well with a fine spray. Leave to drain.

REPOTTING

Potting-on differs from repotting in that is used for plants that have not outgrown their pots or are not required to grow much bigger, but that have been in the same growing medium for several years. To repot a plant, keep in the same size of container and just change the compost.

PRUNING

Herbs grown indoors are pruned in much the same way as outdoor ones. Scented-leaf geraniums, for example, make vigorous annual growth and should be cut back severely just as growth is about to start, otherwise you will be left with untidy, straggly plants. To encourage bushy growth and flowers, your herbs will need to be 'stopped' from time to time. To do this, remove the growing tip or shoot, but only when the plant is actively growing. Left to their own devices some herbs will continue growing until they reach maximum size, which may result in limited flowering and bare stems appearing at the base of the plant. Overcrowding such as this can also encourage disease.

INDOOR HERBS FOR THE KITCHEN

It is worth trying to grow a continuous supply of culinary herbs because fresh herbs always have a better flavour than dried ones. Some varieties can be potted up in autumn or seed can be sown in late summer. They can be kept in a warm greenhouse or conservatory, where they will receive more light. Fennel and tarragon can be over-wintered in pots indoors, and small pieces of the roots of established herbs such as mint, chives and fennel can be lifted in late summer and potted up.

ABOVE **An indoor hanging basket**

INDOOR HANGING BASKETS

Moss gives the most natural look to the baskets when used as a liner, and using soil less composts like peat and coir means that the hanging baskets are considerably lighter, but that they will need watering more often. Plant the taller growing herbs in the top of the basket, with the low-growing and trailing ones around the sides. Regular harvesting will keep the baskets looking tidy.

ABOVE **Parsley is easily grown in an indoor hanging basket**

SOME HERB COMBINATIONS
- A combination of basil, summer savory and marjoram looks attractive.
- Plant chives, parsley and variegated mints together.
- Nasturtiums look splendid with the bright green leaves of parsley.

45

HERBS FOR INDOOR HANGING BASKETS

Aromatic thymes: these make excellent basket fillers. Plant your basket with lemon thyme (*Thymus* x *citriodorus* 'Goldstream'), and the useful kitchen thyme, caraway thyme (*Thymus herba-barona*).

Chives: they make a neat and colourful addition to a hanging basket. They have tubular, grass-like leaves to 4–24in (10–60cm) and round heads of purple flowers from early to mid-summer. They should never be allowed to dry out and are greedy feeders.

Basil: the purple leaves of *Ocimum basilicum* var. *aurauascens* contrast well with the different greens of other herbs. There are many different varieties of basil, such as *O. basilicum* var. *citriodorum* with its green leaves, white flowers and lemon-scent.

Sages: plant rooted cuttings of sage in your basket, trimming them to shape as they grow. There are many types of sage – try purple sage *Salvia officinalis* 'Purpurascens group', for instance, or the wonderful-smelling pineapple sage *Salvia elegans* 'Scarlet Pineapple'.

Chervil *Anthriscus cerefolium* with its lacy leaves, is suitable for over-wintering in a hanging basket. Remove its flowering stems to promote maximum leaf growth.

Nasturtium: 'Double Gleam Mixed' and 'Whirlybird Series' range from scarlet and orange, to yellow and cream. You could also try 'Alaska Mixed', which has variegated foliage.

Mints (*mentha*) come in many different varieties. Try growing ginger mint *Mentha* x *gracilis* 'Variegata' with its bright green and yellow variegated leaves, spicy scent and shorter growing habit. Contain each root in a polythene bag filled with compost, but don't forget to cut drainage holes in the bottom of the bag.

Feverfew grows to a height of 24in (60cm) and can be over-wintered indoors. The leaves are yellowy-green, segmented and aromatic when crushed.

Salad burnet: low-growing and decorative, and holds its cucumber-scented leaves throughout the winter. When the leaves become coarse, cut back the whole plant.

Pot marigold: a decorative plant with splashes of orange flowers. Sowing seed in late summer will provide plants which will over-winter and flower early the following year.

ABOVE **Evergreen purple sage (*Salvia officinalis* 'Purpurascens') with its purple-grey foliage**

HERBS FOR THE KITCHEN

Summer savory: dig out of the garden in late summer, pot up and take indoors. Its leaves have a sharp, spicy flavour. It grows to a height of 4–15in (10–38cm).

Basil: needs warmth and bright light. Sow seed in late summer and place on a sunny windowsill. Water sparingly as the days get shorter. The seedlings will produce fresh growth for many months. Bush basil *Ocimum basilicum* var. *minimum* grows to about 6in (15cm). Sweet basil *Ocimum basilicum* can grow to 24in (60cm). An Italian strain, *Ocimum basilicum* 'Genovese', can be grown for pesto. Purple-leaved basil *Ocimum basilicum* var. *aurauascens* has a very strong flavour.

Chives: lift a clump and split into smaller pieces before potting up and bringing indoors. Water well to settle them in, but water very sparingly afterwards. Trim back the foliage to encourage fresh shoots to develop. They will grow strongly from mid-autumn to mid-spring.

Chervil: grown for its bright green, feathery leaves and aniseed flavour. When growing indoors, it should be given light shade and humidity. It will grow to a height of 12–18in (30–45cm).

Sweet marjoram: grown as a half-hardy annual, will reach a height of 24in (60cm). A winter supply can be provided by potting up established plants in sandy soil in late summer.

RIGHT **The purple-pink pompons of chives (*Allium schoenoprasum*) make a decorative addition to the herb garden**

PLANTING AN INDOOR HERB VEGETABLE RACK

YOU WILL NEED:
Tiered vegetable rack
Polythene sheeting
Gravel
Compost
Selection of herbs

4 Water the plants using a small watering can, and allow them to settle.

1 Line the bottom and sides of each basket with pieces of polythene sheeting. Place a layer of gravel or pebbles over the polythene to provide drainage.

2 Fill each basket with a good quality potting compost.

3 Plant the herbs, making wells in the compost to accommodate them. Firm in well, but gently so that the herbs are not damaged.

5 Position the vegetable rack in a well-lit, draught-free spot.

PLANTING SUGGESTIONS FOR HERB RACKS

TOP TIER
Chervil (*Anthriscus cerefolium*)
Lemon balm (*Melissa officinalis*)
Nasturtium (*Tropaeolum majus* 'Alaska')
Pot marjoram (*Origanum onites*)
Sage (*salvia*)
Spearmint (*Mentha spicata*)
Summer savory (*Satureja hortensis*)
Sweet basil (*Ocimum basilicum*)

BOTTOM TIER
Bush basil (*Ocimum basilicum* var. *minimum*)
Chives (*Allium schoenoprasum*)
Curry plant (*Helichrysum italicum* syn.
   H. angustifolium)
Garlic chives (*Allium tuberosum*)
Parsley (*Petroselinum crispum*)
Thyme (*Thymus vulgaris*)
Tricolour sage (*Salvia officinalis* var. *tricolor*)

MIDDLE TIER
Basil minette (*Ocimum basilicum* 'Minette')
Bay (*Laurus nobilis*) (small rooted cutting)
Borage (*Borago officinalis*)
English lavender (*Lavandula angustifolia*)
Feverfew (*Tanacetum parthenium* formerly
   Chrysanthemum)
Rosemary (*Rosmarinus officinalis*)
Winter savory (*Satureja montana*)

MAINTENANCE
Try to ensure that the rack gets as much sunlight as possible during the day. Feed the herbs with a liquid fertilizer at the intervals recommended on the packet.

Water when necessary, but do not allow the baskets to become waterlogged. Feed the herbs every two weeks with a liquid feed. Spray them occasionally to ensure a good level of humidity. Trim and harvest regularly to keep the plants under control and in good, neat shape.

RIGHT **The crinkled leaves of curly spearmint (*Mentha spicata*)**

49

GROWING HERBS ON WINDOWSILLS

Most herbs will grow well on a sunny windowsill at a temperature of between 55–65°F (13–18°C). They will, however, have a milder fragrance than herbs grown outside. They can be bought in pots. Repot if necessary, leave outside for about two weeks, then bring them indoors. Place on a windowsill, either in a saucer of gravel or on a plastic lined tray. Water once the top of the soil is dry and feed every 10–14 days. A selection of herbs can be planted together in a light, plastic trough, as long as they grow at roughly the same rate.

KITCHEN WINDOWSILLS

Parsley, mint and chives are the toughest herbs, and will tolerate the fluctuations in temperature and humidity and chilling draughts of a kitchen windowsill. Mint will flourish if planted in a separate, large container, and allowed to stand in a saucer or drip tray of water. Fill the bottom third of the pot with crocks or gravel. This ensures that any surplus water is held in this open layer, so that the soil does not become waterlogged and remains aerated. Chives need

less sun but are prone to greenfly invasion when grown in a pot. Dousing the plant well with soapy water should solve the problem.

OTHER WINDOWSILLS

Thyme, marjoram, sage and basil will all flourish on a windowsill in a more stable environment. Herbs prefer one that is draught-free and brightly lit, sunny and with a temperature of around 50–60°F (10–16°C). A south- or south-west-facing windowsill is best during winter. Annuals such as basil, summer savory and sweet marjoram will last longer under such conditions; mint, sage, chives, thyme, parsley and fennel will flourish; and even cuttings of rosemary planted up will thrive. The compost should be kept moist initially, but should remain almost dry during late autumn and winter when growth slows down and light levels reduce. Thyme and sage should be placed nearest to the window to protect shade-loving herbs such as mint, chervil and variegated lemon balm from the sun.

Rosemary, sage and bay will all do well in larger pots, while chives, chervil, thyme and savory are ideal for smaller containers. Thyme, sage, marjoram, scented-leaf geraniums and dwarf lavenders such as *Lavandula angustifolia* 'Nana Alba' enjoy direct sun. Other herbs prefer full sun but a cooler temperature of 60°F (15°C), including dill, savory, chives, rosemary, salad burnet and coriander.

Pots of herbs grown on indoor windowsills are more vulnerable than plants in open ground and need more care. Make sure all containers are adequately drained. Indoor herbs need a drip tray or saucer where excess water can collect. Spray the plants to keep them moist. If air, light, water and nutrients are supplied in adequate amounts, the herbs will flourish.

LEFT **Sweet basil is an ideal candidate for a windowsill**

RIGHT **Rosemary can be grown in a large pot, or makes a good hedge if clipped after flowering**

CHAPTER 3

Choosing and buying herbs

The herbs you grow are a matter of personal taste, although the number and size will be dictated by the space that is available. Whatever you grow, the cultural needs and habits of your plants must come first. So how do you go about choosing which herbs to plant? A good starting point would be to choose a small selection of the well-known favourites, perhaps the 'big five': parsley, chives, mint, thyme and rosemary. These are all easy-care herbs that are simple to grow, will give you a useful stock, and will thrive with comparatively little effort on your part. They are also versatile and useful in the kitchen. Then, as your knowledge of herbs and your expertise grow, you can go on to build up your collection.

ABOVE **A herb rockery established in a sunny spot in the garden**

PARSLEY

Parsley is a biennial native of central and southern Europe, but it grows better if it is treated as an annual. It has curled, crisp, green leaves, and greenish-yellow flowers, which are produced in flat sprays during the second year. First-year plants produce finer, more succulent leaves. The form most commonly grown is the bright green, crimped-leaved *Petroselinum crispum*, although the seed is notoriously slow to germinate. It sometimes takes eight weeks, particularly in wet weather. Germination can be encouraged by soaking the seed in warm water and by pouring boiling water on to the soil before sowing. To ensure a constant supply of this useful herb, seed should be sown twice a year: in early spring, for a summer crop, and again in mid-summer for winter use.

LEFT **Parsley is rich in vitamin C and is best known as a culinary herb**

Parsley likes a fairly rich, non-acid, well-drained soil with plenty of moisture. A certain amount of sun is important, but it will only grow well when its roots are cool, so it should be shaded for part of the day. Dig the soil thoroughly, rake to a fine tilth, and sow the seed thinly in rows 12in (30cm) apart, covering them lightly with soil. When large enough to handle, seedlings should be pricked out to a distance of 8in (20cm). Handle carefully to prevent injuring the roots, which could cause the plants to run to seed. Parsley can also be grown in pots.

Parsley should be kept free from weeds and watered liberally during periods of dry weather. Cut out the flowering stems during the second year – the plant dies after producing seed – to encourage leaf production and lengthen the period of useful life. Pick the foliage regularly, leaving only the green centre of the plant. If you intend to harvest your own seed, leave a few of the plants to flower.

ABOVE **Parsley growing in a terracotta container**

ABOVE **French parsley (*Petroselinum crispum* 'Italian') in flower**

53

MINT

Mints are perennials that can be grown from seed or from root divisions. There are many different varieties, with ovate, lanceolate or ovate-lanceolate leaves and lilac, pink or white flowers.. The best known are applemint *Mentha suaveolens*; Bowles mint *Mentha rotundifolia*; Eau de Cologne mint *Mentha* x *piperita* 'Citrata'; peppermint *Mentha piperita* and spearmint *Mentha spicata*. For flavour, there are really only two: peppermint and spearmint. Peppermint has long, hairy, purplish-green leaves, while spearmint, which is probably the best known of the culinary mints, has narrow, pointed, green leaves and lilac flowers. It usually grows to around 12–39in (30cm–1m).

All mints have a strong, aromatic smell, grow rapidly and spread by underground runners, making them very invasive. They need plenty of water when growing and should also be kept firmly under control. It is best to plant mint in a bottomless bucket or pot, sunk into the soil up to

RIGHT **The decorative, woolly leaves of applemint (*Mentha suaveolens*)**

LEFT **Spearmint is a common culinary mint**

its rim. Mints are good for container planting as they are so invasive; planting in pots keeps them under control. They prefer a moist, rich soil in a shady place, but will grow almost anywhere. Plant different varieties well apart to avoid cross-flavouring.

ROSEMARY

Rosemary *Rosmarinus officinalis* is a perennial, evergreen shrub with long, spiky leaves and a pungent, aromatic scent. Its small, pale blue flowers start to appear in late winter if the weather is mild, and continue until late spring. It will grow outdoors to a height of 6ft 6in (2m) in a sheltered spot, and prefers a light, well-drained soil, with the benefit of some lime – try sprinkling some crushed egg shells around it – in a sunny position. It will grow well against a wall, often growing taller, but tends to grow sideways when it reaches its maximum height.

Rosemary is difficult to cultivate from seed, but if you are successful the plants will be better than those raised from cuttings.

ABOVE **Garden thyme (*Thymus vulgaris*) is most useful in the kitchen**

THYME

There are many varieties of thyme, but *Thymus vulgaris* is the garden or common thyme most often seen in gardens. It is a small, aromatic, shrubby evergreen, hardy perennial up to 18in (45cm) in height. It has woody stems, small, dark green leaves and pale mauve flowers that appear in early summer. It likes a light, well-drained, gravelly soil and a sunny, warm position. It can easily be raised from seed sown in spring. Press the seed into the surface of the compost in a seed tray and transplant seedlings to 12–18in (30–45cm) apart when they are large enough to handle. Thymes are ideal for planting in pots.

Propagation is from cuttings taken in mid-summer with a 'heel' attached, which are then rooted in pots of sandy soil in a cold frame. Tip cuttings can be taken in summer and the plants can also be divided in spring. Plants can also be layered. Cut them well back in mid-summer, and in autumn, to free them of old wood and keep them bushy. Shelter from the cold and wind is important. Thyme is unlikely to survive a hard winter, although it can withstand drought during the summer.

CHIVES

Chives *Allium schoenoprasum* are perennial bulbous plants, and with their pretty, clover-like, pinkish-purple flowers that appear in early to mid-summer and their grass-like foliage, they make lovely garden plants. The tubular leaves, which grow to a height of 4–24in (10–60cm), are evergreen in most climates, but can die back completely in less mild winters.

Chives are easy to grow. Seed can be sown outdoors in spring in drills 10in (25cm) apart and the seedlings thinned to about 6in (15cm) apart. Seed sown outside usually takes more than two weeks to germinate. Seed can also be planted in trays in the greenhouse or directly into pots. Germination under glass at 70°F (21°C) will take around six days. Chive seedlings grow as small, white bulbs with a thin, tapering, green shoot protruding from them. This small bulb produces new bulbs, so several seedlings can be planted together without any fear of overcrowding. Chives like a rich, moist but well-drained soil and prefer a little shade. They grow in clumps and should be divided every two or three years in spring. Always water well after replanting and trim the tops to encourage the growth of new leaves. Remove the flowers to encourage leaf production.

ABOVE **Chives are hardy perennials that will grow in some shade and can be grown in tubs and pots**

ABOVE **Caraway, a biennial, flowers in its second year**

ANNUALS AND BIENNIALS

Annuals and herbs which self-seed (treated as annuals for the purpose of cultivation) are grown from seed each spring.

Biennials are grown from seed and take two years to complete their life cycle. Usually, they flower and produce seed during the second year, but it is possible to keep them growing as perennials for several years simply by removing their flower heads. You can also allow some of the plants to set their seed and produce seedlings, then select the strongest and plant them in a position suited to their needs.

BELOW **Many herbs are very decorative, as well as being useful for culinary purposes**

COMMON ANNUAL HERBS
Anise (*Pimpinella anisum*)
Basil (*Ocimum basilicum*)
Borage (*Borago officinalis*)
Chervil (*Anthriscus cerefolium*)
Common balsam (*Impatiens balsamina*)
Coriander (*Coriandrum sativum*)
Dill (*Anethum graveolens* also *Peucedanum graveolens*)
Nasturtium (*tropaeolum*)
Rocket (*Eruca vesicaria* subsp. *sativa*)
Summer savoury (*Satureja hortensis*)
Sunflower (*Helianthus annuus*)
Sweet marjoram (*Origanum majorana*)

COMMON BIENNIAL HERBS
Angelica (*Angelica archangelica*)
Caraway (*Carum carvi*)
Clary sage (*Salvia sclarea*)
Cotton thistle (*Onopordon acanthium*)
Evening primrose (*Oenothera biennis*)
Mullein (*Verbascum thapsus*)
Parsley (*Petroselinum crispum*), usually treated as an annual
Viper's bugloss (*Echium vulgare*)

ABOVE **Tansy is an invasive perennial that is very easy to grow. If it self-seeds, tiny plants will appear everywhere**

PERENNIALS

Perennial herbs live for several years or more. Most perennial herbs are either shrubs or herbaceous perennials (those considered more for their visual effect). Some can be grown from seed, although they may take three to four weeks to germinate when sown under glass in early spring. Many also grow well when sown in late summer or early autumn as soon as the seeds are ripe, for example sweet cicely and lovage. They are generally sold in pots to plant directly where they are to grow. Shrubby perennials, such as bay, rosemary and sage, should be planted out in early spring or late autumn in humus-rich soil.

Once established, many perennial herbs, for example chives, can be increased by division, or by root runners, for example mint. They can be propagated by several methods, including cuttings. If you increase your own stock in this way, you will not have to buy potted perennials, which will help to cut down your expenses considerably.

In moderate and cold climates, most perennial herbs will die back at the end of the summer and virtually disappear into the soil, their root systems remaining underground. If you live in a cold area, protect your plants over

COMMON PERENNIAL HERBS
Fennel (*Foeniculum vulgare*)
Hyssop (*Hyssopus officinalis*)
Lemon balm (*Melissa officinalis*)
Rue (*Ruta graveolens*)
Sweet cicely (*Myrrhis odorata*)
Tansy (*Tanacetum vulgare*)

ABOVE **Lemon balm is a useful ingredient of potpourri**

winter with a layer of organic mulch such as spent mushroom compost, seaweed, dried lawn clippings or garden compost. Mulches will not only protect them from frosts, but will also provide valuable nutrients. In spring, the herbs will reappear and should be mulched again to encourage leaf growth and later flowers.

ABOVE **Dividing clumps of mint (*Mentha*) using a spade**

ABOVE Lungwort or pulmonaria appears early in the spring

HERBS FOR SHADE

Many herbs will grow in either sunny or shady places. A shady part of the garden, perhaps under a tree, seems hardly conducive to growing herbs, but many herbs, particularly those with medicinal uses, will tolerate or even prefer shade.

Herbs grown in shade do flower, but usually very early in the year, and their blooms are often of poor quality. Shade reduces the range of herbs that you can grow, but there is a wide

HERBS FOR HEAVY SHADE
Evening primrose (*Oenothera biennis*)
Lily of the valley (*Convallaria majalis*)
Pennyroyal (*Mentha pulegium*)
Sweet violet (*Viola odorata*)
Valerian (*Valeriana officinalis*)

variety of culinary, ornamental and other herbs that will flourish in shady spots. A heavily shaded herb patch will most happily have woodland perennials as its inmates. It will be at its brightest from late winter to early spring. The first to flower will be the woodland hellebores *helleborus* and lungwort *Pulmonaria officinalis*, followed by violet and woodruff, then lily of the valley, Jacob's ladder *Polemonium caeruleum* and Solomon's seal *Polygonatum multiflorum*.

LEFT Ginger mint will flower readily in damp soil

DAMP SHADE

Some herbs enjoy a position with damp shade: ginger mint *Mentha x gracilis* 'Variegata' for example. Given these conditions, ginger mint will bear long, red stems with lilac flowers between its green and gold leaves from early summer to autumn. Both creeping pennyroyal *Mentha pulegium* 'Cunningham Mint' and upright pennyroyal *Mentha pulegium* will become a carpet of scented leaves along paths and banks. Other herbs such as elecampane *Inula helenium* and bugle *Ajuga reptans* will flourish in a moist, shady position.

HERBS FOR PARTIAL SHADE

Other herbs will flower later and prefer a dappled shade, for example angelica. Lovage also prefers some shade to develop its large leaves, and sorrel thrives in shade, producing better leaves in consequence. Light or gold variegated herbs such as golden marjoram, golden sage and variegated lemon balm prefer dappled shade, and also benefit from the sun not scorching their foliage. Chervil and borage are also fond of shady places.

MORE HERBS FOR PARTIAL SHADE
Figwort (*Scrophularia nodosa*)
Foxglove (*Digitalis purpurea*)
Lady's mantle (*Alchemilla mollis*)
Musk mallow (*Malva moschata*)
Rocket (*Eruca vesicaria* subsp. *sativa*)
St John's wort (*Hypericum perforatum*)
Sweet cicely (*Myrrhis odorata*)

ABOVE **A small rocket plant (*Eruca vesicaria*) which can grow to a height of 24–39in (60cm–1m)**

LEFT **Borage enjoys a shady position**

ABOVE Tall herbs look majestic in a herbaceous border

TALL AND MEDIUM HERBS

There is a range of architectural, statuesque herbs that are ideal for the herbaceous border. When planning a herb border, plant the tallest herbs at the back in clumps rather than in rows for a cottage garden effect. If planting an island bed that can be viewed from all round, plant them in the centre to prevent them from overshadowing the smaller plants. Tall herbs can be slotted in anywhere in the garden, to hide a fence or wall, or placed in the vegetable garden, for example. Tall herbs need plenty of space around them, so allow about 2ft (60cm) between them when planting.

LEFT Yellow-flowering mullein grows to 6ft 6in (2m)

ABOVE **Sorrel is a useful plant for the middle of a herb border, or even a flower bed**

COMMON TALL HERBS

Angelica (*Angelica archangelica*) can reach 3–8ft (1–2.5m)

Chicory (*Cichorium intybus*) will grow to 4ft (1.2m) but usually needs staking

Elecampane (*Inula helenium*) can reach 10ft (3m)

Fennel (*Foeniculum vulgare*) will grow to 6ft 6in (2m) but should not need support because of its upright habit

Lovage (*Levisticum officinale*), can reach 6ft 6in (2m); may need staking despite its strong, upright growth

Mullein (*Verbascum thapsus*) will grow to 6ft 6in (2m)

HERBS OF MEDIUM HEIGHT

Agrimony (*Agrimonia eupatoria*)

Basil (*Ocimum basilicum*)

Borage (*Borago officinalis*)

Caraway (*Carum carvi*)

Comfrey (*Symphytum officinale*)

Coriander (*Coriandrum sativum*)

Cotton lavender (*Santolina chamaecyparissus*)

Curry plant (*Helichrysum italicum* syn. *H. angustifolium*)

Dill (*Anethum graveolens* also *Peucedanum graveolens*)

Feverfew (*Tanacetum parthenium* formerly *Chrysanthemum*)

Horehound (*Marrubium vulgare*)

Hyssop (*Hyssopus officinalis*)

Lavender (*lavandula*)

Lemon balm (*Melissa officinalis*)

Mint (*mentha*)

Marjoram (*origanum*)

Pot marjoram (*Origanum onites*)

Rampion (*Campanula rapunculus*)

Rue (*Ruta graveolens*)

Sages (*salvia*)

St John's wort (*Hypericum perforatum*)

Sorrel (*Rumex acetosa*)

Southernwood (*Artemisia abrotanum*)

Sweet cicely (*Myrrhis odorata*)

RIGHT **Golden feverfew is a beautiful, decorative herb that grows to a height of about 24in (60cm)**

LOW-GROWING HERBS

These do best at the front of the garden so they will get plenty of sun. They are also useful for edging beds or paths; you could try white flowering lavender *Lavandula angustifolia* 'Nana Alba', which is very low-growing at just 6–12in (15–30cm). To enclose a herb garden, a hedge of clipped box is neat and attractive. One of the best varieties of lavender for hedging is *Lavandula angustifolia* 'Royal Purple', with its deep purple flowers and compact habit, growing to a height of 32in (80cm).

Paths can be softened by cascading thymes, chamomile, Corsican mint and creeping winter savory. Pennyroyal and sweet marjoram are also low-growing, although their flower stems can rise above the main level of the plant. Chives and parsley make attractive edges for beds and borders, and rock hyssop, at only 8–12in (20–30cm) tall, is ideal for planting in paving or for rock gardens.

PROSTRATE HERBS

Prostrate herbs grow rampantly to produce a dense carpet of foliage and often a mass of flowers. They can be used to suppress weeds, soften harsh features and cover areas of bare earth. They are effective in the herb garden, and there are varieties for both sunny and shady areas. Many varieties are suitable for paths, but should be enclosed by small pieces of brick or slate to prevent them encroaching on herb beds.

ABOVE **Low-growing Corsican mint**

LOW-GROWING PLANTS (UP TO 18IN / 45CM)
PERENNIALS
Bistort (*Polygonum bistorta*)
Calamint (*Calamintha officinalis*)
Chives (*Allium schoenoprasum*)
Roman chamomile (Chamaemelum nobile 'Flore Pleno')
Sweet marjoram (Origanum majorana)
Thyme (thymus)
Winter savory (Satureja montana)

ANNUALS AND BIENNIALS
Anise (*Pimpinella anisum*)
Basils (*ocimum*)
Cumin (*Cuminum cyminum*)

Creeping thyme *Thymus serpyllum* will cover paths and paving slabs with a scented carpet of flowers and foliage. It will soften cracks, smother banks and thrive on the tops of walls. Corsican mint *Mentha requienii* will flourish under shrubs and trees, as will woodland herbs such as woodruff *Galium odoratum* with its spreading mass of starry, white flowers.

HERB THEMES

Over the centuries, herbs have been used in many different ways. These offer an open-ended source of ideas for herb themes, which can range from a Biblical Herb Garden to one that grows salad herbs. Herbs adapt to a number of themes and designs, but whatever you decide upon, always establish where your garden will be sited and plan it to scale on paper before you start.

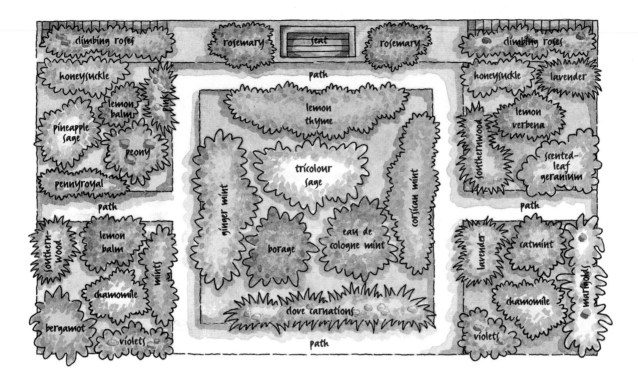

ABOVE **A ground plan of a potpourri garden**

POTPOURRI GARDEN

Plant a potpourri garden and you will have the scents of summer all winter long. Try growing peonies for their strong red flowers and pinks for their truly wonderful scent. Lavender also makes a lovely aromatic addition, as does *Eau de Cologne* mint that goes so well with the lemon herbs. Violets are ideal for their perfume and colour as is lemon balm with its clean fresh smell. As a backdrop to this type of garden, grow wonderfully fragrant roses and sweetly scented honeysuckle.

PLANTING SUGGESTIONS

Alecost (*Tanacetum balsaminta*)
Bergamot (*Monarda didyma*)
Borage (*Borago officinalis*)
Carnations (*Dianthus chinensis* 'Strawberry Parfait')
Catmint (*Nepeta cataria*)
German chamomile (*Matricaria recutita*)
Ginger mint (*Mentha x gracilis* 'Variegata')
Japanese honeysuckle (*Lonicera japonica*)
Lavender (*lavandula*)
Lemon balm (*Melissa officinalis*)
Lemon verbena (*Aloysia triphylla*)
Pennyroyal (*Mentha pulegium*)
Peony (*Paeonia officinalis*)
Pineapple sage (*Salvia elegans* 'Scarlet Pineapple')
Rose, climbing (*Rosa* 'Rosy Mantle')

DYER'S GARDEN

If you are interested in spinning and weaving and dyeing your own yarn, what better than to grow your own dye herbs so that you can mix your own colours?

ABOVE **The petals of pot marigold produce a pale yellow dye, earning it a place in a dyer's garden**

ABOVE **Common gypsyweed or gipsywort (*Lycopus europaeus*) will yield a brown dye**

PLANTING SUGGESTIONS

REDS
Dyer's bugloss (*Alkanna tinctoria*)
Dyer's madder roots (*Rubia tinctorum*)
Lady's bedstraw (*Galium verum*)
Rue (*Ruta graveolens*)
Sorrel (*Rumex acetosa*)

BLUES
Elder tree (*Sambucus nigra*) – use berries
Privet (*Ligustrum vulgare*) – use berries
Woad (*Ivatis tinctoria*) – use leaves
Indigo (*Indigofera tinctoria*)
Juniper (*Juniperus communis*) – use berries

GREENS
Ivy (*Hedera helix*)
Lily of the valley (*Convallaria majalis*)
Nettles (*Urtica urens*)
St John's wort (*Hypericum perforatum*)
Tansy (*Tanacetum vulgare*)

BRIGHT YELLOWS
Agrimony (*Agrimonia eupatoria*)
Broom (*Cytisus scoparius*)
Golden rod (*Solidago virgaurea*)
Lily of the valley (*Convallaria majalis*)
Tansy flowers (*Tanacetum vulgare*)
Thyme (*thymus*)

SOFTER YELLOWS
Apple (*Malus sylvestris* var. *domestica*)
Daffodil (*narcissus*)
Dandelion (*Taraxacum officinale*)
Pear (*Pyrus communis* var. *sativa*)

MEDICINAL GARDEN

Medicinal herbs were widely used in the past, but no one should ever attempt to treat themselves with medicinal herbs without first seeking advice from a qualified herbalist. The number and variety of herbs that you plant will depend on the size of the garden. Do not overcrowd the beds. Tall herbs are planted towards the centre as the garden will be viewed from all sides.

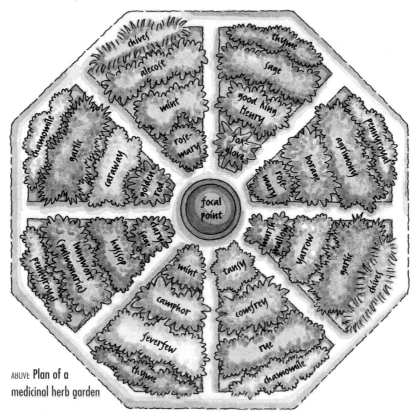

ABOVE **Plan of a medicinal herb garden**

PLANTING SUGGESTIONS

Agrimony (*Agrimonia eupatoria*)
Borage (*Borago officinalis*)
Caraway (*Carum carvi*)
Catmint (*Nepeta cataria*)
Chives (*Allium schoenoprasum*)
Clary sage (*Salvia sclarea*)
Comfrey (*Symphytum officinale*)
Feverfew (*Tanacetum parthenium* formerly
  Chrysanthemum)
Foxglove (*Digitalis purpurea*)
Garlic (*Allium sativum*)
German chamomile (*Matricaria recutita*)

Goldenrod (*Solidago virgaurea*)
Good King Henry (*Chenopodium bonus-
  henricus*)
Hyssop (*Hyssopus officinalis*)
Lungwort (*Pulmonaria officinalis*)
Marsh mallow (*Althaea officinalis*)
Mints (*mentha*)
Pennyroyal (*Mentha pulegium*)
Rosemary (*Rosmarinus officinalis*)
Rue (*Ruta graveolens*)
Sages (*salvia*)
Tansy (*Tanacetum vulgare*)

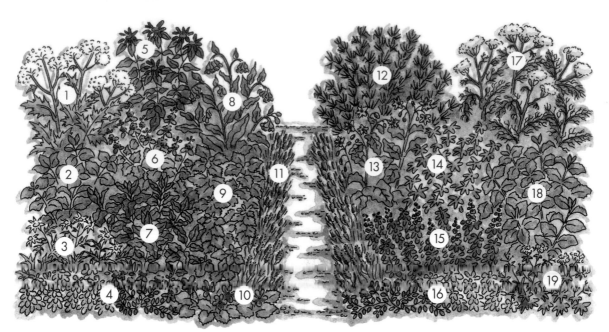

TEA GARDEN

Growing herbs to make herbal teas or tisanes is not difficult. They make delicious drinks served hot, cold or iced. Some are slightly stimulating, many are tonics. They are a pleasant alternative to tea and coffee and do not contain tannin or caffeine. Before drinking a herbal tea, always check with a qualified herbal practitioner, as people suffering from certain medical conditions should not drink particular teas.

PLANTING SUGGESTIONS

Angelica (*Angelica archangelica*)
Fennel (*Foeniculum vulgare*)
Hyssop (*Hyssopus officinalis*)
Lemon balm (*Melissa officinalis*)
Lemon verbena (*Aloysia triphylla*)
Mints (*mentha*)
Ginger mint (*M. x gracilis* 'Variegata')
Peppermint (*M. piperita*)
Rosemary (*Rosmarinus officinalis*)
Sages (*salvia*)
Thymes (*thymus*)

ABOVE **Plan of a tea garden**

KEY TO ILLUSTRATION:
1 Angelica
2 Basil
3 Chamomile
4 Thymes
5 Bergamot
6 Ginger mint
7 Sage
8 Comfrey
9 Lemon balm
10 Violets
11 Lavender
12 Rosemary
13 Borage
14 Lemon verbena
15 Hyssop
16 Thymes
17 Fennel
18 Peppermint
19 Woodruff

EVERLASTING HERB GARDEN

Many herbs can be harvested and dried to bring their rich scents and colours into the house during the long winter months. The following selection will remind you of summer days and, when dried, they can all be used in flower arrangements. They dry easily, retaining both their shape and colour.

ABOVE **Dog rose (Rosa canina) adds colour to any garden**

SHAKESPEAREAN HERB GARDEN

The Elizabethans valued herbs highly and Shakespeare mentioned them frequently in his plays. He wrote of 'hot lavender' and 'rosemary for remembrance', as well as rue which he called 'the sour herb of grace'.

ABOVE **Heartsease was popular in Shakespearean times**

PLANTING SUGGESTIONS

Bergamot (*Monarda didyma*)
Borage (*Borago officinalis*)
Cotton lavender (*Santolina chamaecyparissus*)
Hops (*Humulus lupulus*)
Lavender (*lavandula*)
Love-in-the-mist (*Nigella damascena*)
Poppies (*papaver*)
Purple leaved sage (*Salvia officinalis* 'Purpurascens')
Rosemary (*Rosmarinus officinalis*)
Safflower (*Carthamus tinctorius*)
Tansy (*Tanacetum vulgare*)

PLANTING SUGGESTIONS

Bay (*Laurus nobilis*)
Caraway (*Carum carvi*)
Chamomile, lawn (*Chamaemelum nobile* 'Treneague')
Cowslip (*Primula veris*)
Fennel (*Foeniculum vulgare*)
Heartsease (*Viola tricolor*)
Iris (*Iris florentina*)
Lavender (*lavandula*)
Lemon balm (*Melissa officinalis*)
Marjoram (*origanum*)
Myrtle (*Myrtus communis*)
Parsley (*Petroselinum crispum*)
Pinks (*dianthus*)
Rose (*rosa*)
Rosemary (*Rosmarinus officinalis*)
Rue (*Ruta graveolens*)
Salad burnet (*Sanguisorba minor*)
Savory (*satureja*)
Thyme, creeping (*Thymus serpyllum*)
Violet (*Viola odorata*)
Wild honeysuckle (*Lonicera periclymenum*)
Wormwood (*Artemisia absinthium*)

CHAPTER 4

Harvesting and preserving herbs

Herbs have great ornamental value, but are really intended for use. All but the evergreens, however, can be freshly picked only for a limited period of the year, so they need to be preserved if they are to be used all year round. The best time to harvest varies from plant to plant. Careless harvesting and storing will spoil all the hard work put into growing the plants, so make sure you know which parts to pick: usually the leaves and stems, but sometimes the seeds, flowers or roots.

Herbs can be harvested when they are well established, with enough growth not to be adversely affected. Usually the tips of the stems are harvested to encourage the plant to make more growth. The aim is to preserve all of the herb's volatile oil, which gives it its flavour, and as much natural colour as possible. The essential oils, which are concentrated in the leaves, are not as strong during winter, so do not over-pick outside the growing season because the herb will not be renewing itself.

LEFT **Herbs hanging to dry on a kitchen dresser**

ABOVE **A trug containing freshly harvested herbs, where they will not sweat, or get crushed or bruised**

SELECTING HERBS FOR HARVESTING

Evergreen herbs like sage, thyme, rosemary and winter savory can be picked throughout the year (although winter savory should be given the chance to harden off before winter comes), and the fresh leaves of all herbs can be picked for immediate use throughout the growing season.

Harvest only one species of herb at a time. Plants growing under optimum conditions can be harvested in mid-summer and again in the autumn. The shrubby sages, the thymes and tarragon will usually bear two crops. Much depends on the weather, and herbs are always at their best after a dry summer. Whatever the climate, herbs must be harvested before they reach full maturity and begin to die back.

If gathering herbs from the wild, make sure that your plant identification is correct as some herbs are poisonous. If you are not absolutely certain, leave well alone. You also need to be sure that the herbs you collect are not contaminated in any way by pollutants such as pesticides or herbicides or, if near a road, by

lead from the atmosphere. Remember that most countries have protected species, so check that you are within the law before picking.

ABOVE **The aromatic leaves of Jerusalem sage (** *Phlomis fruticosa* **)**

69

ABOVE **Coriander seeds harvested ready for air drying**

WHAT, WHEN AND HOW OF HARVESTING

Always harvest herbs on a dry day. If they are cut when wet, not only are they difficult to handle, but mildew may set in before they can be preserved and the crop will be lost. Pick when the plants are at their most potent, in the morning when they are just open and after the dew has dried, but before the heat of the sun. Never harvest more herbs than you can deal with quickly. If you cannot begin the preserving process straight away, strip off the lower leaves and place the stems in a jug of cold water in a cool, dark place. Herbs that are left lying around quickly lose their flavour.

LEAVES AND STEMS

Use a sharp knife to cut the stems of small-leaved herbs; larger leaves can be picked by hand. Handle as little as possible to avoid bruising, and remove any browned or damaged leaves. Harvest leaves just before the plant comes into flower when their flavour is best. Cut flowers for preservation just as they are fully open.

Cut back perennial herbs by about one-third and annuals to the bottom leaves. Do not cut all the plant's growth if you want fresh leaves later in the season. Herbs tend to heat up quickly, so do not place them in a bag or they will begin to sweat and get crushed and bruised. Lay them on a trug or wooden tray. If the leaves are muddy or dusty wash them gently, then shake them to remove as much moisture as possible. Work quickly so that the scents and flavours are preserved.

Upright thymes can be bunched together, held with one hand, and then cut with a sharp knife about 3in (7.5cm) from the base. Cut angelica stems for candying in early summer.

FLOWERS

Cut flowers for preservation just as they become fully open. Cut lavender and lady's mantle in full bloom, or the flowers may fall apart when fully dry. Flowers do not improve in colour once picked, and they must be picked at the correct time if they are not to shrivel or drop.

SEEDS

Caraway, coriander, dill, fennel and lovage should be harvested for their seed, which should be gathered when the seed heads turn brown. Tap the seed heads daily; if the seeds begin to fall, the herb is ready to be gathered. Do not let the seeds fall and scatter, and do not leave them in the wet or they will go mouldy.

ROOTS AND BULBS

Harvest roots in autumn when the tops of the plants are beginning to wither and die down. Scrub the roots as soon as they are lifted, remove fibrous parts, and cut into small pieces before drying.

DRYING HERBS

The aim of drying herbs is to remove the water content but change them as little as possible. Herbs are about 70 per cent water; the secret is to remove it as quickly as possible without losing any of the volatile oils. Leaves lose about 75 per cent of their water; roots a little less. Effectively, you are dehydrating them to a point at which mould and bacteria can no longer develop. Many herbs keep their flavour when dried; some flavours even improve by becoming more concentrated. Do not wash the leaves unless absolutely necessary, keep them out of the sunlight, and dry them in the shortest time possible. Treat flowers in exactly the same way. If flowers are dried correctly, they will keep their colour, the leaves and stems will remain green, and there will be no problem with mildew. Some of the best flowers to dry are borage, chamomile, elder, honeysuckle, marigold petals, meadowsweet, rose petals and violets.

Always dry herbs in the dark. If they are dried in light, natural or otherwise, they will lose both quality and colour as the volatile oils evaporate in the heat. They also need a good circulation of air around them and good ventilation to carry away the humidity that drying plants create. The temperature at which to dry varies according to the requirements of individual herbs, but should remain constant. Between 24–26°C (75–80°F) is reasonable, but it should be a little higher for the first 24 hours if possible.

Herbs are dry when they are brittle enough to snap and crackle when pressed. Fully dried leaves will part from the stems and they will crumble, not fall into dust. They will also have a lovely aromatic smell, and will keep for about nine months to a year, although lovage, mint and marjoram will keep for longer. Bear in mind, though, that if they are kept too long, they will lose their flavour, colour and scent.

ABOVE **A variety of air-dried herbs, ready to be stored in airtight containers**

AIR DRYING

Air drying is the traditional way of preserving herbs. It relies on air to dry out the moisture in the plants.

Stems and leaves

Remove damaged leaves and woody stems from the cut herbs and tie the stems with twine in small bundles – about 10–12 stems to a bunch. Tie them loosely with a slip knot so that the knot can be tightened as the stems shrink. Don't pack the leaves too tightly and don't mix the different species. Strip off any lower leaves that could get caught up in the twine. The drying period of each herb will vary; 7–10 days is average, but this will depend upon the thickness of the leaves. Never allow herbs to dry until the leaves collapse on contact.

For herbs such as mint, rosemary, sage, bay, savory and thyme, rig up a line of string or twine in a warm, dry, airy place away from direct sunlight. Hang the herbs upside down so that air can circulate around them, using a clothes peg or paperclip to secure them to the line. Excluding humidity is also very important, so do not use anywhere that is likely to become damp: steamy kitchens and bathrooms, for example.

On a warm, dry day, herbs can be left outside suspended from a clothes airer, away from direct sunlight. Herbs can also be dried in an airy, well-ventilated garden shed, an attic or even a cupboard under the stairs. If you use a cupboard, leave the door open slightly to allow dampness to escape as the herbs are drying. Alternatively, make trays from pieces of muslin stretched over wooden frames and then placed

ABOVE **A line of herbs being air dried in a warm, dry garden shed, away from direct sunlight**

LEFT **Chamomile flowers can be air dried in a net bag**

completely, and shake each bag occasionally. Alternatively, arrange flower heads still on their stems at varying heights so that the air can circulate more easily around them. Or place petals and small flowers between sheets of newspaper to dry, or spread them out on muslin-covered frames.

The length of time it takes for a flower to dry will depend upon its moisture content and the moisture in the atmosphere. When the flower stem is dry and rigid, the flower is ready for storage. The petals will feel dry and 'papery'.

When cutting lavender, lay the stems in a flat basket with all the flower heads together. This will make bunching easier. Never leave cut lavender in bundles on a table because the moist heat generated will spoil the perfume. When you are air drying lavender, place a dust sheet underneath the bunches to catch any falling flowers.

on supports to allow air to circulate underneath. Herbs can also be spread on trays with perforations that will allow the air to circulate, or on slatted shelves. Turn them for several weeks until quite dry. You may also use shallow boxes lined with paper, again turning frequently.

Low-growing herbs such as summer savory, woodruff and centaury should be dried whole with their stems. For large herbs such as sweet cicely and lovage, strip off the leaves before drying, and dry the thick, fleshy leaves of herbs such as comfrey, sage and coltsfoot individually.

Flowers and petals

Suitable flowers for air drying include fennel, yarrow, dill, chives, feverfew, cornflowers, chamomile, lady's mantle, rosebuds, lavender and marigolds.

Hang flowers and petals in small quantities in netting bags – the ones in which fruit and vegetables are sold in supermarkets. These come in different mesh sizes. Never fill them

ABOVE **Bunches of lavender tied, labelled and ready to dry**

ABOVE **Caraway seeds ready for harvesting. Do not allow them to become over-ripe**

SEED HEADS

Cut the stems of seed heads of herbs such as fennel, dill, coriander, cumin and caraway, tie in bunches and hang upside down with the seed heads suspended in paper bags. When dry, the seeds will 'crack' when touched, and should crumble between the fingernails. Remove them from the paper bags and store.

ROOTS

Spread sliced or cut pieces of root on drying trays and leave in a warm, dark place, like an airing cupboard, until they are hard and brittle.

OVEN DRYING

Herbs can be dried in an oven, but do this gently, as too much heat will also dry out the essential oils, thus removing the scent or flavour. Never place plant material in a lit gas oven because the volatile oils in the herbs can cause a fire hazard. A gas oven should always be turned off before plant material is placed in it, with the door left ajar.

Bunch and tie the herbs and then string them from the oven racks or spread them out on foil on the racks. Set the oven at the lowest setting of 225°F (110°C). Leave the door open. Turn them frequently to allow moisture to escape. Depending on the herb and the season, drying can take several hours.

The leaves of tough-stemmed herbs such as bay should be removed before they are placed in the oven. These can be individually positioned on the racks to dry. Large sage leaves can also be dried individually, while smaller ones can be bunched. Rosemary and thyme leaves can be dried in bunches. Roots of herbs such as horseradish *Armoracia rusticana*, angelica *Angelica archangelica* and marsh mallow *Althaea officinalis* can also be dried in an oven.

STORING IN THE REFRIGERATOR

First wash the herbs and dry them gently on kitchen paper, handling them carefully so that they do not bruise. Place them in a plastic bag and store in the refrigerator, but not near the freezer compartment. They will also keep for several days if placed in a covered container.

ABOVE **Jerusalem sage should not be dried in the microwave – for microwave drying, choose common sage**

MICROWAVE DRYING

Microwave drying speeds up the process of drying without affecting the flavour of the herbs, and is successful because of the short processing time involved. It is, however, difficult to dry large quantities of plant material in this way, as only limited amounts can be dried at one time.

Place small bunches of herbs or individual fleshy leaves on kitchen paper in a single layer in the microwave, making sure that no two pieces are touching, and process on a low power for about 2–3 minutes. The timing will depend on the moisture content and thickness of the leaves, so drying can take longer.

Leaves of herbs such as rosemary, sage and lavender microwave well, as do the flower clusters of chamomile, lady's mantle, tansy, yarrow and marjoram. When using the microwave, check your plant material every 30 or 40 seconds once it is almost ready. Remove leaves and flowers as soon as they are crisp and papery. Do not leave them for even a few seconds too long or they will become too brittle. Remember that microwaves vary in power, so it will be necessary to experiment with drying times. When drying aromatic herbs, keep a close eye on them because the volatile oils could vaporize and catch fire.

MICROWAVING SAGE LEAVES

1 Select about 10–12 leaves of uniform size.

2 Place leaves on a piece of kitchen paper, trimming it to size if necessary, and making sure that the leaves do not touch.

3 Microwave on 450W for 4–5 minutes, depending on the size of the leaves, turning them half-way through the process. Stop the microwave from time to time to check them.

4 Remove the leaves from the oven and test them for dryness and crispness.

5 Store the dried leaves in an airtight container until ready to use.

TEN GOLDEN RULES FOR HARVESTING AND DRYING

1 Always harvest herbs in the morning once the dew has dried and before the heat of the sun has had the chance to evaporate the volatile oils.

2 Never pick herbs on a wet day or after rain when they will still be damp.

3 Only harvest herbs that are established, in prime condition, and that are at their most potent. Never over-pick.

4 Use a sharp knife to avoid the possibility of bruising, and avoid handling as much as possible.

5 Only harvest the amount of herbs you are able to deal with quickly. Place any that cannot be dealt with immediately in water in a cool, shady spot.

6 Never place cut herbs in a plastic bag. They will sweat and get bruised.

7 Separate herbs into small bunches. Keep each species and variety separate to avoid cross-flavouring. Label and date each batch.

8 Never dry herbs that have damaged leaves or flowers or that are suffering from any disease or pest infestation.

9 Dry all herbs in the shortest time possible, with a moderate heat, good air circulation and adequate ventilation.

10 Dry all plant material in a dark place.

ABOVE **Air dried marigolds ready for storage. The petals are removed and stored in an air-tight jar**

STORING DRIED HERBS

Dried herbs should be stored as quickly as possible so that they do not re-absorb any moisture from the atmosphere. If this happens, they will deteriorate and become musty. Strip the leaves from the stems and store whole, crumbling just before use. Place them in air-tight containers in a cool, dark place. Dark glass jars with a screw top are preferable to plastic ones which will make the dried material sweat. If you notice moisture on the inside of the containers, the herbs are not completely dry. Take them out, lay them out on paper, and allow them further drying time.

Sage, rosemary and thyme can be left on their stalks. Bay leaves should be left whole, and all seeds and flowers placed in air-tight containers. Check regularly for any mould and throw the herbs away if any is found. Always label and date any containers you use so that you know their age exactly.

FREEZING

Freezing is an ideal method of preserving herbs with a delicate flavour and foliage and which do not dry successfully: chervil, salad burnet and sweet cicely, for example. Once harvested, freeze the herbs as quickly as possible in small batches. Herb sprigs can be frozen in plastic freezer bags or plastic containers – this way they tend to be less mushy when defrosted. Make sure that the containers are airtight to prevent other frozen foods from becoming tainted by the herbs' aroma. Label and date all containers.

Freezing is a popular method of preserving culinary herbs. Frozen herbs do not have such a long storage life as air-dried plants, but they can be kept for about six months. Parsley, savory, mint, marjoram, sorrel, chives and fennel all freeze well. Once herbs have been frozen, they tend to lose their texture, so you will not be able yo use them as a garnish. For long-term storage, blanch the herbs by dipping them first in boiling water and then in cold water, before placing them in freezer bags.

ABOVE **Preparing sprigs of parsley for freezing**

FREEZING HERBS IN ICE CUBES

Herbs can also be frozen as ice cubes.

Single mint leaves, borage flowers and marigold petals all freeze well in ice cubes, as do chopped parsley and chives.

1 Chop the leaves and place them in ice trays. Fill the trays with water and freeze.

2 Store in plastic bags when frozen.

DECORATIVE USES FOR HERBS

Herbs can be kept supple by preserving them in a glycerine solution. This changes the colour of the foliage, gives it added sheen and ensures that it lasts indefinitely. The stems in the solution take up the mixture and carry it to all parts of the plant: you can actually see the glycerine working its way up the leaf veins and spreading over the whole leaf. The water gradually evaporates and the plant cells retain the glycerine. Different varieties of leaves are affected in different ways: the pattern of the fleshy leaves of clary and nasturtium, for example, becomes more pronounced, while those of bay and rosemary become slightly darker and retain their perfume.

YOU WILL NEED:
Bottle of glycerine
Water: hot, but not boiling
Bottle for mixing the solution
Large jar or vase
Cotton wool
Dry containers: vases, jars
Hammer
Herbs

1 Prepare the herbs by stripping off any low-growing leaves and crushing the ends of any woody stems, such as those of sage and bay, with a hammer.

2 Mix one part glycerine with two parts very hot water in a bottle. Screw on the top and shake thoroughly. Pour the solution into a container, such as a large jar or vase, to a depth of about 2in (5cm).

NOTE Herbs preserved in this way are used solely in decorative arrangements. They should never be eaten or used in cooking.

3 Completely submerge the stem ends of the herbs in the glycerine and water and leave the container in a dry place away from strong light for at least three days. The time needed will vary from herb to herb and larger pieces, such as branches of bay or rosemary, may take longer. Do not use branches that are too tall and remove any damaged leaves.

4 Dip a piece of cotton wool into the glycerine solution and coat any thick leaves with it. This will prevent the leaves from curling and the process can be repeated at regular intervals. Replenish the glycerine solution if necessary.

5 Remove the stems from the solution as soon as the leaves have changed colour and stopped taking in liquid. The material should now be soft, supple and shiny.

6 Wash and dry the stems and store upright in dry containers. Do not discard the glycerine solution as it can be used again. Store it in a covered bottle and reheat before use.

ABOVE **Soft, supple herbs after soaking in glycerine**

CANDYING HERB FLOWERS

Some herb flowers can be candied to preserve them. Try violets, lavender, rosemary, sage, mint and bergamot. Lemon balm leaves can also be candied. Remember to check that the flowers you use are edible, as many are not.

YOU WILL NEED:
Violets, gathered on a sunny morning after the dew has dried
1 egg white
Caster sugar
Whisk
Tweezers (optional)
Wire rack or baking tray
Greaseproof paper

1 Whisk the egg white in a bowl until frothy.

2 Dip the violets in the egg white, one by one, so that each bloom is well coated. Use tweezers if you wish. Shake off any surplus egg white.

3 Dip the damp violets individually in the caster sugar.

4 Place on a wire rack or baking tray lined with greaseproof paper, positioning them so that they do not touch each other.

5 Place in an open oven with the temperature on the lowest setting, and dry slowly until they are completely dry and brittle.

6 Remove from the oven and store them between sheets of greaseproof paper in an airtight container.

HERB FLOWER SUGARS

Herb flowers can be made into flower sugars by pounding the flowers with three times their own weight of caster sugar and storing in glass jars away from direct light. Suitable flowers for this method are violets, lavender, jasmine, rosemary and rose petals.

ABOVE **Store candied angelica in an airtight jar**

CANDIED ANGELICA

Pencil-thin stems of angelica harvested in early summer can be preserved in sugar. Cut the stems into 3–4in (7.5–10cm) lengths, boil in a little water until tender, drain and peel off the outer skin. Simmer again until bright green. Dry the stems on kitchen paper and weigh them. Place in a shallow dish, and add an equal weight of sugar, sprinkled over the stems. Leave for two days. Boil the mixture, making more syrup if necessary, for ten minutes. Drain, then spread the stems on a rack to dry thoroughly.

PRESERVING IN OIL AND VINEGAR

In medieval times, herbs and flowers were preserved in oil or vinegar and this method is still used today.

FLOWERS

Use a good white wine vinegar for flowers such as lavender, mint, basil, thyme and rosemary, and a cider vinegar for darker flowers such as sweet violets and red roses. Remove all stalks, green parts and white heels of the petals before using and steep the scented flowers in the vinegar, or oil, for three to four weeks. Leave the bottles to stand on a sunny windowsill, turning them at regular intervals to allow the sun to release the flowers' natural oils. Give them a good shake each day.

Scented flowers go well with oils such as sunflower or safflower, while aromatic herb flowers complement a richer oil: hazelnut or olive, for example. It is best to use your flower oils within three months; although they will last longer – up to six months – if the flowers are removed. Try lavender, jasmine and rose petals in a light oil, and flowering herbs such as mint, marjoram, thyme, dill and fennel in an olive or hazelnut oil.

ABOVE **Basil can be preserved in good-quality olive oil**

ABOVE **Bottles of herb oils and vinegars**

ABOVE **Herb oils should be stored away from sunlight**

sunlight for two to three weeks, shaking every day. Strain off the leaves and repeat the process until you have the strength of flavour you require. Strain the oil into bottles, add a sprig of the herb, and seal tightly. Label and date.

LEAVES

The leaves of tarragon, basil, dill, fennel, mint, summer savory and salad burnet make excellent vinegars. Wash and dry the leaves, pack them into a wide-necked jar and pour in the vinegar. White wine vinegar is best for basil, tarragon and salad burnet and cider vinegar for mint. Screw the lid on tightly and stand the jar on the windowsill. Shake it every day. If, after 10 days, the taste is not strong enough, take out the leaves, strain the vinegar and add fresh leaves. Repeat the process until you are satisfied with the strength of the flavour, then strain the vinegar into bottles and add a sprig of the herb before sealing. Label and date.

Herb oils can be made from the leaves of basil, tarragon, thyme, fennel and rosemary. Crush the leaves, place in a wide-necked jar and pour over the oil. Leave the jar in the

MORE IDEAS FOR PRESERVING

1 Use the old-fashioned method in which layers of herbs, for example basil leaves, are alternated with layers of coarse salt in a wide-necked jar. Pour olive oil over and seal the jar tightly. It will keep in the refrigerator for several weeks.

2 Keep dried bay leaves on a long stalk and store in a tall, glass jar in a dark corner of the kitchen.

3 Preserve herb leaves and flowers by pressing in flower presses. Use to make pictures, greetings cards and bookmarks.

4 Soak nasturtium seeds overnight in salt water, pickle in vinegar, and eat them as you would capers.

5 Make bouquets garni by tying dried parsley, thyme and a bay leaf in muslin. Store in an airtight jar and use in stews, casseroles and soups and for marinades.

RIGHT **Bouquet garni**

SECTION TWO

CHAPTER 5

A–Z plant directory

This directory does not claim to be an exhaustive list of herbs, but it does include a good selection that will allow you to create an attractive and varied herb garden, wherever you live. Individual herbs are listed alphabetically with all the information you should need to get started. Popular varieties are listed after each herb.

NAMING OF PLANTS

If the description of the herb is all in italics, this is a naturally-occurring plant that has been discovered growing in habitat. For example, in *Angelica archangelica*, Angelica is the genus name and Archangelica is the species name. This is a plant that was originally discovered growing in Europe and Asia, and is therefore a true species. Botanists may find slight variations, so if you see the terms f. or var. or subsp. they describe naturally-occurring forms, varieties and subspecies.

If, however, you see a description like *Agastache foeniculum* 'Alabaster', it tells you that the plant is a cultivar, and that plant breeders and hybridizers have been selecting and crossing plants to produce a distinctive plant which they can name. If you see a description that has 'xxxx' after any name in this plant directory, you will know that it is a cultivar rather than a true species.

HARDINESS RATINGS

The information given is based on UK Royal Horticultural Society data, but is on the cautious side. If you are not prepared to take any chances, follow the hardiness rating to the letter. Otherwise, there is a great deal of leeway. Raised beds, good drainage, south-/south-west facing borders and planting against a house wall all give plants a better habitat – so be prepared to experiment. If you cannot bear the thought of losing your most valued plants, keep back-ups by taking cuttings or dividing the plants and growing spares, perhaps in a different part of the garden.

Half-hardy: down to 32° F/0° C
Frost-hardy: down to 23° F/–5° C
Fully hardy: down to 5° F/–15° C
(FT) Frost tender

SAFETY WARNING:

Many plants can be harmful, both if eaten and as skin irritants, or because they are allergens and will aggravate asthma, eczema and other auto-immune disorders. Do not eat them unless you are certain that they have a culinary use. Be wary of skin contact, especially in bright sunlight. Tell children never to eat anything from the garden unless you have given it to them!

NAME: **AGRIMONY**
AGRIMONIA EUPATORIA
FAMILY: **ROSACEAE**

Type: Hardy perennial

USDA zone: Z7

Description: Agrimony is an upright herb with a long, black root and a red stem that bears attractive grey-green cinquefoil leaves in alternate large and small pairs. It has racemes of apricot-scented, star-shaped, yellow flowers on tapering spikes.

Height: 12–24in (30–60cm).

Where to grow: In an ornamental border or in the middle of an informal herb bed or herb garden. Agrimony likes full sun and a well-drained soil, but it will tolerate some shade. It will also flourish in short grass and is often found in hedgerows and grasslands.

How to grow: Sow seed in a prepared seed bed in spring or autumn. Established roots can be divided in autumn.

Flowering period: Flowers in summer, followed by bristly, burr-like fruits that stick to clothes.

Maintenance: Leave relatively undisturbed, but keep the soil moist.

Harvesting and uses: Gather leaves just before the plant flowers, and pick the flowers well before the formation of seed heads Both can be used fresh or dried. Roots can be lifted, dried, grated and added to pot-pourri. The herb is also grown for a bright yellow dye.

Pests and problems: Generally trouble free.

Other species and varieties: Hemp agrimony *Eupatorium cannabinum* is a tall-growing perennial found in damp grassland and marshes. It has trifoliate leaves and dull, lilac flowers in late summer and early autumn. Water agrimony *Bidens tripartita*, found on the edges of ponds or ditches, has an erect stem marked with brown spots and a profusion of leaves. Brownish-yellow flowers are followed by burr-like fruits.

NAME: **ANGELICA**
ANGELICA ARCHANGELICA
FAMILY: **UMBELLIFERAE**

Type: Hardy biennial

USDA zone: Z7

Description: Angelica is a moisture-loving native of damp meadows and riverbanks in northern Europe and Asia. It is a handsome plant with large, glossy, deeply-indented, bright green leaves. Its round, hollow, purplish stem, branched near the top, grows from a reddish-brown rootstock. The whole plant has a scent reminiscent of juniper or musk.

Height: 3–8ft (1–2.5m).

Where to grow: Angelica can be grown in sun or partial shade but benefits from a mulch if planted in full sun. Plant at the back of the herb garden because of its height. It will grow well in a large container.

ABOVE **Angelica stems can be candied, and the leaves can be used in pot pourri mixes**

How to grow: Sow the fresh, newly ripened seed in autumn in drills 1in (2.5cm) deep in rich, fertile soil. Thin the seedlings to 6in (15cm) apart. Otherwise, sow in early spring. Germination can be erratic, but it usually takes 2–3 weeks. The large, oval ridged seeds can also be sown in autumn, in pots on a sunny windowsill, and over-wintered. Sow 2 or 3 seeds to a pot, keep them warm and moist, and transfer them to their growing position outside in early summer. Store the seed in an airtight jar in the refrigerator for planting later. Angelica will self-seed prolifically if it is allowed to flower. It can be also propagated by the off-shoots thrown out when the two-year-old plant is cut down for its stems in spring. Plant 2–3ft (0.6–1m) apart.

Flowering period: Heads of numerous, greenish-white flowers are produced in mid-summer, in large, terminal, compound umbels that emit a honey-like perfume. These are succeeded by oblong fruits, composed of two yellow winged seeds.

Maintenance: Angelica is quite difficult to grow, so keep the soil moist after sowing to aid germination. It dies after flowering, but its life can be prolonged by cutting off the flower heads before they form, or by cutting it down to ground level in late autumn.

Harvesting and uses: Young stems from two-year-old plants can be candied in the spring. The leaves can be dried for pot-pourri mixtures.

Pests and problems: An infestation of aphids that spread viral diseases and cause damage can sometimes be found on Angelica. It can sometimes cause skin allergies.

Other species and varieties: Wild Angelica *Angelica sylvestris* is a smaller, less striking variety with similar, but weaker, properties. There are about 30 varieties of Angelica that are no longer cultivated.

NAME: ANISE
**   *PIMPINELLA ANISUM***
FAMILY: UMBELLIFERAE

Type: Half-hardy annual
USDA zone: Z10–11
Description: Anise is an attractive, feathery annual with a ridged, round, branching stem and small, star-like, white flowers. Leaves broad and jagged at the base, but finely cut and feathery further up. Both the flowers and seed smell of aniseed.
Height: About 18in (45cm).
Where to grow: Enjoys a light, dry soil and full sun. It will also thrive in pots on a sunny patio, and between paving stones.
How to grow: Sow the aromatic, egg-shaped seeds in early spring or when all danger of frost has passed, in drills 9in (22.5cm) apart. Thin to 4in (10cm) when the seedlings are 2in (5cm) high. Seeds can also be sown directly into window boxes and pots. Anise needs careful attention to grow well. Seeds take some time to germinate and require fairly high temperatures.
Flowering period: Clusters of white flowers in late summer are followed, if the weather is warm, by brown seeds. The seeds ripen about four weeks after flowering, provided temperatures are high.
Maintenance: Keep young plants well weeded. When the seed heads become heavy, support each plant with a wigwam of small canes.
Harvesting and uses: Collect the seed heads as they start to colour, or cut down the whole plant and dry it slowly it in a warm place. Store the seeds in an airtight jar and use to flavour liqueurs, cakes or bread. The leaves can also be eaten in salads.
Pests and problems: The seeds may fail to ripen if the weather is too cold.
Other species and varieties: Star anise *Illicum verum* a native of China, produces star-shaped seeds.

NAME: **ANISE HYSSOP**
AGASTACHE FOENICULUM
FAMILY: **LABIATAE**

Type: Moderately hardy perennial
USDA zone: Z10–11
Description: Anise hyssop is a North American mint that dies down in the winter. The pointed, nettle-shaped leaves have pale undersides and serrated margins and a distinct aniseed smell. It has spikes of purplish-blue flowers.
Height: 3ft (1m).
Where to grow: Anise hyssop is happy to grow in almost any type of soil and copes readily with light shade. Likes sunny, but cool, weather. Primarily ornamental, it is good for attracting bees.
How to grow: Sow seed under cover in early summer. It can also be propagated from softwood cuttings taken in summer, and by root division in spring. It will also self-seed.
Flowering period: The purplish-blue flowers bloom from mid- to late summer.
Maintenance: Anise hyssop can be short-lived, so increase your supply by taking cuttings every two to three years.
Harvesting and uses: Harvest the aniseed-flavoured leaves in spring and summer and add them to meat and salad dishes. Use fresh or dried as a flavouring.
Pests and problems: Mildew can be a problem in hot summers.
Other species and varieties: *Agastache foeniculum* 'Alabaster' is a dense, bushy plant that bears white flowers. It grows to a height of 18–24in (45–60cm).
Korean mint *Agastache rugosa* is a short-lived, upright perennial with a mint-like aroma. It has small purple flowers and pointed leaves, and grows to a height of 3–4ft (1–1.2m).

RIGHT **Mature sweet basil (*Ocimum basilicum*)**

NAME: **BASIL**
OCIMUM BASILICUM
FAMILY: **LABIATAE**

Type: Half-hardy tender annual
USDA zone: Z10–11
Description: Basil is an attractive, branching herb with large, juicy, bright green leaves and creamy white flower spikes. It has a warm, spicy aroma.
Height: 24in (60cm).
Where to grow: Plenty of sun is essential, so a warm, sheltered corner of the herb garden is ideal. Basil is also good on a sunny windowsill. Make sure the pot is kept at a temperature of 50–60°F (10–16°C).
How to grow: Basil originated in India where it is perennial, but in cooler countries it is better

treated as a half-hardy annual. It enjoys a rich, well-drained, light soil, kept moist. Sow the seed under glass in early spring. Basil does not transplant well, so sow just one or two seeds to a small pot and plant out complete, without disturbing the rootstock. Seed can also be sown in succession throughout the summer for a good supply. It can be raised on a sunny windowsill and moved into the herb garden in mid-summer. As it is an herbaceous plant, cuttings can be taken from mature plants. Root non-flowering side shoots in pots during summer for winter use.

Flowering period: The white flower spikes appear in the late summer. They should be cut off as they form to produce strong and bushy plant growth.

Maintenance: Avoid overwatering the seedlings as they are prone to 'damping off'. Pinch out the tips of shoots at regular intervals to prevent flowering. Cut the herb several times throughout the growing season to allow it to produce fresh leaves. Cut at least 4–6in (10–15cm) above the ground. Move the plant indoors in autumn, and it should flourish up to Christmas, or even later.

Harvesting and uses: The tops can be picked, chopped and used to flavour savoury dishes. Chop fresh leaves into omelettes, or use in soups, salads and sauces. Dry the leaves whole in a warm place. When dry, rub them between your hands and store them in an airtight jar. Preserve freshly-harvested whole sprigs in olive oil or wine vinegar to be used later in salad dressings.

Pests and problems: Basil can become rather straggly. To prevent this, snip off the top shoots when the plant is about 6in (15cm) high. Slugs and caterpillars enjoy the young leaves.

Other species and varieties: There are more than 50 types of basil. Popular varieties include bush basil *Ocimum basilicum* var. *minimum*, a bushier, more shrub-like variety with smaller leaves than *Ocimum basilicum*. Lemon basil *Ocimum citriodorum* has bright green leaves and strong lemon scent. Lettuce-leaved basil *Ocimum basilicum* var. *lactucafolium*, is another native of India. It has crinkled leaves up to 3in (7.5cm) across. Purple basil *Ocimum basilicum* var. *aurauascens* 'Dark Opal' is a decorative red-leafed variety that is ideal for growing in the ornamental border.

LEFT **A selection of basils can be grown together and placed near the kitchen door**

NAME: **BAY**
LAURUS NOBILIS
FAMILY: **LAURACEAE**

Type: Half-hardy perennial

USDA zone: Z10–11

Description: Bay is a slow-growing evergreen aromatic plant with shiny, leathery, dark green leaves that emit a pungent, spicy aroma when broken. The young stems are purple-brown, becoming woody and grey as they mature.

Height: 10–50ft (3–15m).

Where to grow: Bay enjoys a rich, moist, well-drained soil. Plant in full sun and protect from the wind. Can be grown in a pot and clipped into shape. It will thrive for years without repotting.

How to grow: Take cuttings of 3–4in (7.5–10cm) long shoots of half-ripened stems in late summer, pot, and place under a cloche or in a propagator – bottom heat is always helpful. Place young plants in a prepared and sheltered bed in a well-drained warm soil. Stems can sometimes be layered in autumn. Viable seed is vitually impossible to obtain.

Flowering period: Small, yellow flowers appear in the axils of the leaves in late spring, followed by round, purplish fruits.

Maintenance: Can be clipped back as a decorative shrub. The traditional shapes for container-grown bays are bush, pyramid and mop-head.

Harvesting and uses: Pick the leaves at any time. Their aroma is greatly improved if they are dried. Hang a branch in an airy spot for about two weeks, or press the leaves flat. Store dried leaves in airtight jars away from light. Leaves can be used to flavour stews, meat dishes and casseroles, and must be cooked for a long time to release their strong flavour. Bay leaf is an essential ingredient of bouquet garni.

Pests and problems: Bay is vulnerable to severe frosts. It will usually survive the winter, but it is safer to grow it in a pot that can be

ABOVE **Bay can be grown in pots and tubs and can be clipped into attractive shapes**

moved to a sunny greenhouse or conservatory. It may be attacked by suckers (psyllids), which causes the leaf margins to become thickened, curled and yellowed.

Other species and varieties: Canary Island bay *Laurus canariensis* has reddish-brown branches, and the colour sometimes extends into the leaves.

WARNING: Bay belongs to the laurel family and could be mistaken for the poisonous cherry laurel. Identify carefully before using.

ABOVE **Lemon bergamot (*Monarda citriodora*) originates in the southwestern US**

NAME: BERGAMOT
MONARDA DIDYMA
FAMILY: **LABIATAE**

Type: Hardy perennial
USDA zone: Z9–11
Description: Bergamot, also known as Bee Balm, is a decorative, aromatic herb. The whole plant has a wonderful lemon-orange scent. It has slightly-toothed, hairy leaves and whorls of scarlet, white, pink or mauve flowers.
Height: 2–3ft (60–90cm).
Where to grow: Bergamot favours a rich, moist soil and a sunny, sheltered position. It likes a cool root run, so it flourishes best in partial shade. Try planting it in the middle of a border or along a path. It is not suitable for growing indoors.
How to grow: Work some compost or manure into the soil before planting. Sow the seed or plant in late spring and early summer. Propagate by seed, by dividing its fibrous roots in spring, or by taking cuttings in autumn.

Divide the roots every other year, but replant only the outer shoots as the inner part of the established plant tends to die.
Flowering period: Flower clusters on the ends of upright stems from early summer onwards. These are very attractive to bees.
Maintenance: Ensure that the roots are kept moist but do not let the plant become waterlogged. Mulch in dry weather.
Harvesting and uses: Harvest the young leaves before the flowers form and use them fresh or dried. Whole plants can be collected for drying during the flowering period, and the flowers retain their colour well. Fresh flowers can be used to decorate salads and the leaves to flavour omelettes, fish and chicken dishes.
Pests and problems: Young bergamot leaves are attractive to slugs, and often become covered in mildew in autumn.
Other species and varieties: Lemon bergamot *Monarda citriodora*, a native of North America, is used to flavour tea.
Wild bergamot *Monarda fistulosa* is a medicinal plant with purple (or, occasionally, white or pink) flowers.

NAME: BISTORT
POLYGONUM BISTORTA
FAMILY: **POLYGONACEAE**

Type: Fully hardy
USDA zone: Z7
Description: Bistort is an ornamental plant with triangular leaves and dense spikes of tiny, pale pink flowers.
Height: 3ft (1m)
Where to grow: Enjoys a rich, moist, preferably acidic soil and will grow in full sun or partial shade. Try growing in a shady border or a corner of the herb garden.
How to grow: Sow seed in a cold frame in late spring, using a soil-based compost.

90

Propagate also by naturally-rooted runners, or by root division in early autumn to prevent it from becoming invasive.

Flowering period: Tiny, pink flowers in summer followed by hard nutlets.

Maintenance: Mulch in autumn and spring. Give a general fertilizer in spring. Trim back growth in autumn. Lift and divide the plants every two–three years.

Harvesting and uses: Harvest the leaves in autumn. Young leaves can be used in salads.

Pests and problems: Birds often eat the seeds.

Other species and varieties: *Polygonum bistorta* 'Superbum' is an attractive, widely grown variety with showy pink flowers that grows to a height of 24–30in (60–75cm).

NAME: BORAGE
BORAGO OFFICINALIS
FAMILY: BORAGINACEAE

Type: Hardy annual
USDA zone: Z9–11
Description: An attractive herb with large, rough, hairy leaves and brilliant blue flowers, it is a great favourite with bees.
Height: 12–39in (30cm–1m).
Where to grow: Borage thrives in a light, fairly rich soil and a sheltered, sunny position, but needs lots of sun to bring out the flavour. It makes an excellent companion plant when it is grown with squash, tomatoes and strawberries. Small plants can be grown indoors to provide leaves throughout the winter.
How to grow: Borage is propagated by seed only, sown at intervals throughout the summer. Sow the seeds ¼in (6mm) deep, thinning to 12in (30cm) apart. Once it is established, borage will self-seed freely. Seed can also be sown in pots.
Flowering period: Star-like, bright blue flowers with black anthers appear in drooping clusters from early summer onwards.

ABOVE **The stunning, blue star-shaped borage (*Borago officinalis*) flowers attract bees into the garden**

Maintenance: Remove unwanted seedlings and keep the young plants free from weeds. Will need pruning on occasions to keep it tidy.
Harvesting and uses: Young leaves, with their cucumber taste, can be used in salads. Flowers can be candied, scattered over salads, or frozen into ice cubes for summer drinks.
Pests and problems: Both aphids, which spread viral diseases, and downy mildew, which is encouraged by cool, wet springs and autumns, can affect the plants.
Other species and varieties: *Borago officinalis* 'Alba' has the same cucumber-flavoured leaves but pure white flowers.
Borago pygmaea is popular for its clear blue flowers, but cannot be used as a substitute for *Borago officinalis*.

ABOVE Clipped box can be used to make an attractive edging for a mixed herb bed

NAME: **BOX**
BUXUS SEMPERVIRENS
FAMILY: **BUXACEAE**

Type: Hardy evergreen
USDA zone: Z7
Description: Slow-growing evergreen shrub with closely packed oval, leathery leaves, shiny and dark green above, paler underneath. Small greenish-white flowers.
Height: 16ft (5m).
Where to grow: Box enjoys a rich, light soil in full sun, although it will tolerate light shade. It also prefers a neutral or alkaline, well-drained soil. Suitable for planting in large pots and good for topiary.
How to grow: In spring or autumn, place box plants 8in (20cm) apart for hedging. Repot young plants in spring. Propagate by softwood or semi-ripe cuttings planted in a mixture of peat or peat substitute and sand. Seed cases open to eject small black seeds which often root where they fall.
Flowering period: Small greenish-white flowers in mid-spring. Both male and female flowers bloom on the same plant.
Maintenance: Keep well-watered and feed

annually in spring. Trim to encourage bushy growth. Topiary and hedges can be trimmed into shape in summer. The plant can be pruned right back when dormant.
Harvesting and uses: Harvest the leaves in early spring before the plant flowers. The leaves yield a red dye, and both bark and leaves are used for infusions. Box is also used in homeopathic remedies. Boxwood is used to make rulers and mallet heads.
Pests and problems: Throughout the summer, box can be attacked by box leaf suckers. The leaves can also be affected by rust or leafspot.
Other species and varieties: Cape box *Buxus macowanii* has similar properties and is used in South Africa.
Buxus sempervirens 'Kingsville Dwarf', an American cultivar, grows a mere ½in (1cm) each year and is often used as a bonsai specimen.
Buxus sempervirens 'Suffruticosa' is ideal for hedging and topiary.

WARNING: All parts of box are toxic if eaten. The plant can cause allergies and skin irritations.

NAME: **BUGLE**
AJUGA REPTANS
FAMILY: **LABIATAE**

Type: Fully-hardy perennial
USDA zone: Z7
Description: Bugle is a short, prostrate ornamental herb with rosettes of coarse, shiny green leaves and spikes of deep blue, occasionally pink or white, flowers.
Height: 6in (15cm).
Where to grow: Bugle prefers a moist soil in sun or partial shade. It can be used as ground cover, planted in the wildflower garden, and

grown in borders, and will also thrive beneath a hedge if compost is added.

How to grow: Sow seed in trays in spring or autumn, covering very sparingly with compost. Thin when large enough to handle. Can also be propagated by division in spring or autumn, and from naturally-rooted runners.

Flowering period: Spikes of flowers in spring and early summer.

Maintenance: Mulch in autumn and spring until the plant is established. Give a light dressing of fertilizer in spring. Cut back dead flower heads.

Harvesting and uses: The plants are usually harvested in summer and are used fresh in medicinal preparations like ointments and medicated oils. The whole herb can be cut down in summer and dried.

Pests and problems: Seed germination is slow and erratic. Can be attacked by mildew.

Other species and varieties: *Ajuga reptans* 'Variegata' is a less-vigorous variety with variegated, light green foliage, that is ideal for growing in containers and for the rock garden. *Ajuga reptans* 'Burgundy Glow' is a colourful evergreen, ground cover plant with light bronze and pink foliage.
Ajuga reptans 'Atropurpurea' has dark purple leaves and dark blue-purple flowers.

ABOVE **When ripe, the caraway (*Carum carvi*) fruits split into two crescent-shaped, dark brown seeds**

NAME: CARAWAY
CARUM CARVI
FAMILY: UMBELLIFERAE

Type: Hardy biennial
USDA zone: Z9–11
Description: Caraway is a dainty, relatively low-growing plant with feathery, carrot-like leaves. It produces umbels of small, white flowers followed by aromatic fruits.
Height: 8–24in (20–60cm).
Where to grow: Caraway enjoys a well drained, fertile soil and a sunny site sheltered from cold winds. It can also be grown in pots.

How to grow: Sow the seed in spring out of doors where the plants are to flower, about 2in (5cm) deep, and 6–8in (15–20cm) apart, in rows at the same distance apart. Caraway also self-seeds prolifically.

Flowering period: Flowers in early summer, in the second summer after sowing.

Maintenance: Leave undisturbed, except for weeding, until the year after sowing. If the established plants die down in winter, cut them level with the ground so that they will grow again the following spring.

Harvesting and uses: Harvest young roots and use as a vegetable. Gather the ripe seeds at the end of the second summer and dry in small bunches. Use in seedcake, caraway cake, to flavour confectionery and bread, and in soups and stews. They are an important ingredient of Asian and Indian cookery.

Pests and problems: Winter waterlogging can kill the plants, and their taproots are easily damaged if transplanted.

Other species and varieties: Normal species only is available.

ABOVE **Catmint is easily grown from seed**

NAME: **CATMINT**
NEPATA CATARIA
FAMILY: **LABIATAE**

Type: Hardy perennial
USDA zone: Z9–11
Description: Catmint is an attractive ornamental plant with branched stems, grey-green leaves and white flowers with mauve markings that grow in whorls.
Height: 1–3ft (30cm–1m).
Where to grow: Enjoys a light, moist, well-drained soil and a position in full sun.
How to grow: Sow seed where the plants are to grow in autumn or spring. Thin the seedlings when they are large enough to handle. Plants should reach flowering size in their first year. Roots can be divided in spring, and stem-tip or softwood cuttings taken in spring or summer.
Flowering period: Flowers summer to autumn.
Maintenance: Mulch lightly in early spring and autumn. Cut back after flowering to provide a second harvest. Cut the whole plant back to ground level in autumn.

Harvesting and uses: Gather leaves and flowering stems and use fresh or dried. Dried leaves are often used to stuff cat toys. Leaves can be infused for a mint-like tea.
Pests and problems: Powdery mildew can attack and damage the leaves. Cats love catmint and will eat it and roll in it.
Other species and varieties: *Nepata cataria* 'Citriodora' is a fully hardy, lemon-scented variety that grows to 1–3ft (30cm–1m).

NAME: **CENTAURY**
CENTAURIUM ERYTHRAEA SYN.
ERYTHRAEA CENTAURIUM
FAMILY: **GENTIANACEAE**

Type: Hardy annual
USDA zone: Z9–11
Description: Centaury has smooth, shiny, pale green leaves and umbels of pink flowers with yellow centres, arranged in clusters.
Height: 12in (30cm), sometimes less.
Where to grow: Will grow in most garden soils, but prefers sandy, neutral to alkaline ones. It is happy in sun or semi-shade and can often be found growing wild in damp meadows. Good in a herb rockery.
How to grow: Sow the seed in autumn or spring where the plants are to grow, barely covering them with soil. It also self-seeds.
Flowering period: Flowers appear in summer.
Maintenance: Virtually maintenance free.
Harvesting and uses: Harvest the plant at flowering time and dry it quickly. Centaury can be used medicinally and is also an ingredient of vermouth.
Pests and problems: None.
Other species and varieties: American centaury *Sabatia stellaris* is a biennial herb found in wet areas and marshes.
Seaside centaury *Centaurium littorale* can be found on sand dunes, but is smaller, with narrower leaves and paler but larger flowers.

ABOVE **Roman chamomile (*Chamaemelum nobile*) is a mat-forming evergreen perennial with solitary flowers**

NAME: CHAMOMILE – ROMAN
CHAMAEMELUM NOBILE FORMERLY
ANTHEMIS NOBILIS
FAMILY: COMPOSITAE

Type: Hardy perennial
USDA zone: Z9–11
Description: Chamomile has green, feathery leaves and daisy-like flowers with creamy-white petals. The whole plant has a wonderful, fruity, apple-like scent.
Height: Rarely more than 6in (15cm).
Where to grow: Camomile likes a light but rich soil. It thrives in a sunny window box, between paving stones, on slopes, or around garden seats, and is an ideal patio plant. Both the flowering and non-flowering varieties make attractive ground cover.
How to grow: Chamomile can be grown from seed or from its small rooted runners. Plant these in spring about 4in (10cm) apart. They will soon spread to form a neat area. Divide plants in spring or autumn, and take 3in (7.5cm) cuttings from side shoots in summer.
Flowering period: Summer and autumn.

Maintenance: Minimal, apart from weeding between the creeping, tufty leaves. Chamomile lawns must be cut by hand with shears or scissors during the first year. In the second year, a mower with blades set high can be used.
Harvesting and uses: Pick flower heads at any time, dry and store in airtight containers. Both fresh and dried flower heads make a calming infusion. Dried flower heads can be used in pot-pourri, herb cushions, and sachets.
Pests and problems: Chamomile lawns can look straggly, with gaps that allow weeds to take root. It attracts snails, and is also subject to aphid attacks and sooty mould.
Other species and varieties: *Chamaemelum nobile* 'Treneague' is a non-flowering variety, used for lawns. It will die down in winter, exposing the soil.
German chamomile (*Matricaria recutita* syn. *Matricaria chamomilla*) is an annual variety grown by herbalists for its healing oil.
Double flowered chamomile *Chamaemelum nobile* 'Flore Pleno' has creamy-white double flowers and apple-scented leaves.

NAME: CHERVIL
ANTHRISCUS CEREFOLIUM
FAMILY: **UMBELLIFERAE**

Type: Hardy annual
USDA zone: Z9–11
Description: Umbels of small, white flowers
and small, feathery, green leaves that take on
a faint pink-purple hue during late summer.
Height: 12–18in (30–45cm).
Where to grow: Chervil enjoys a fertile, moist,
light and well-drained soil. Avoid extreme heat
and cold and provide partial shade. It is a
good indoor plant.

ABOVE **Chervil can be eaten fresh in salads, and the dried seed heads
look good in floral arrangements.**

How to grow: Sow in shallow drills where it is
to grow, as it does not like being transplanted.
Cover lightly with soil and keep moist;
germination is fast. Thin seedlings to 6in
(15cm) apart when they are large enough to
handle. Sow the seed out of doors several
times from late spring to mid-summer for a
succession of leafy plants. Can also be sown
in late summer for an indoor winter supply.
Flowering period: Small, white flowers appear
from early to late summer.
Maintenance: Make sure the site is kept moist.
Allow some plants to flower and produce
seeds to ensure a self-seeding supply.
Harvesting and uses: Leaves can usually be
cut 6–8 weeks after sowing. Use fresh, as
drying destroys the slightly peppery, parsley-like
flavour. Chervil is delicious with egg dishes,
sauces and salads. Dried seed heads can be
used in floral arrangements.
Pests and problems: Chervil will run to seed in
hot, dry conditions.
Other species and varieties: Bulbous chervil
Chaerophyllum bulbosum grows in the wild
and has tuberous roots.
Rough chervil *Chaerophyllum tenuilentum* is a
close relative of bulbous chervil.

NAME: CHIVES
ALLIUM SCHOENOPRASUM
FAMILY: **LILIACEAE**

Type: Hardy perennial
USDA zone: Z9–11
Description: A bulbous, perennial herb with
dense, hollow tufts of grass-like leaves growing
from clusters of small bulbs, and pompon
heads of purple-pink flowers in summer.
Height: 6–12in (15–30cm).
Height: 24in (60cm).
Where to grow: Chives enjoy full sun but will
tolerate some shade. The herb will flourish in
most soils, but prefers a moist, well-worked,

ABOVE **Chives are an attractive addition to any herb garden, and give a delicate onion flavour to many dishes**

slightly acid loam with plenty of humus added. It makes a neat edging for borders and will also thrive in pots.

How to grow: Sow the seed in spring or autumn, 0.5in (1cm) apart, either in outside drills where they will germinate in about 14 days, or in seed trays under glass where germination will take around six days. When they are large enough to handle, transplant two or three seedlings together at 8in (20cm) intervals. Rotate several clumps for a succession of leaves. Chives take about a year to produce leaves that are suitable for harvesting. Established plants can be lifted either in spring or autumn and divided into clumps of bulbs. Ideally, this should be done every three years, as they tend to become 'tired'.

Flowering period: Flowers appear in summer, followed by seeds that turn black when ripe.

Maintenance: Once the plants are established, the soil should be kept well watered, particularly in dry weather.

Harvesting and uses: Trim the leaves close to the ground. Chop and sprinkle on salads, or use in scrambled eggs and omelettes.

Pests and problems: May be attacked by onion fly if planted too close to leek or onion beds. Can be affected by rust, particularly in mild areas. Good companion plants because their pungency deters carrot root fly and helps to lessen black spot on roses.

Other species and varieties: Garlic or Chinese chives *Allium tuberosum* are extremely decorative, with larger, flatter leaves and white star-like flowers that appear in the autumn.

ABOVE Clover (*Trifolium pratense*) makes marvellous ground cover and its clove-scented flowers are a favourite for bees

---

NAME: **CLOVE CARNATION/CLOVE PINK**
DIANTHUS CARYOPHYLLUS
FAMILY: **CARYOPHYLLACEAE**

Type: Perennial
USDA zone: Z9–11
Description: Lanceolate, grey-green leaves and small, deep pink to purple flowers.
Height: 8–20in (20–50cm).
Where to grow: Clove carnation prefers an open sunny position in well-drained, alkaline soil. It can be grown in a sunny spot indoors.
How to grow: Grow as short-lived perennials. Sow seed in spring and thin or transplant to 1ft (30cm) apart. Take cuttings, divide roots or layer the plants in late summer.
Flowering period: Flowers appear in summer.
Maintenance: Do not mulch, as it can cause stem base rot. Dress lightly with fertilizer in spring. Cut off dead flower heads. Discard the plants after about three years or when they become straggly.
Harvesting and uses: Pick the flowers once they have opened and air dry or preserve using silica gel. The fresh petals can be crystallized. Flowers can be infused in wine vinegar or in almond oil for a sweet oil.

Pests and problems: Prone to leaf-attacking insects, thrips, virus and leaf spots.
Other species and varieties: Chinese pink (*Dianthus chinensis* 'Strawberry Parfait') is a very compact plant that is good for containers. *Dianthus superbus* is a fringed pink variety.

NAME: **CLOVER/REDCLOVER/PURPLECLOVER**
TRIFOLIUM PRATENSE
FAMILY: **LEGUMINOSAE**

Type: Perennial
USDA zone: Z9–11
Description: Clover is a short-lived plant with long-stalked, three-lobed leaves and abundant, fragrant, purplish-pink flowers.
Height: 8–24in (20–60cm).
Where to grow: Clover likes a neutral, moist, well-drained soil. It enjoys a sunny site but can withstand very low temperatures. It is suitable for the wildflower garden.
How to grow: Sow seed in spring in rows or in patches. Plants can be divided in spring.
Flowering period: Purplish pink flowers borne in globose heads from late spring.
Maintenance: Virtually none.
Harvesting and uses: Flowers and leaves can be gathered and cooked as a vegetable or used raw in salads. The dried leaves and flowers have medicinal uses. The flowers make good wine, and also yield a yellow dye.
Pests and problems: None.
Other species and varieties: *Trifolium pratense* 'Broad Red' is an agricultural variety that has been widely grown since the 17th century. *Trifolium pratense* 'Susan Smith' is grown as an ornamental, and is prized by gardeners for its variegated leaves.
Whiteclover *Trifolium repens* is a creeping variety with larger leaves and fragrant white or pink flowers.

NAME: **COLTSFOOT**
TUSSILAGO FARFARA
FAMILY: **COMPOSITAE**

Type: Hardy perennial
USDA zone: Z9–11
Description: Coltsfoot has bright yellow, dandelion-like flowers that appear before the hoof-shaped leaves. The leaves have green veins that grow bigger throughout the summer.
Height: 12in (30cm).
Where to grow: Coltsfoot needs sunshine for most of the day and moist soil in full sun is ideal. It is ideal for planting in an uncultivated section of the herb garden, because it is a wild plant that is found in ditches and on wasteland. To contain its rapid spread, it can be grown in containers.
How to grow: Sow seed in spring in moist soil. Transplant seedlings when they are large enough to handle. Can be propagated by division in autumn. Root cuttings can be taken in spring and autumn, but they must be kept moist when planted.
Flowering period: Flowers in early spring.
Maintenance: Virtually none, but lift and divide the plants every two years to prevent them from becoming invasive.
Harvesting and uses: Pick, cut up, and dry the leaves in summer. Flowers should be gathered before fully open. Both leaves and the flowers can be used fresh and the flowers can be made into wine. *Tussilago* means cough-destroyer and this is the principal medicinal use of the herb.
Pests and problems: Can be very invasive.
Other species and varieties: Normal species only available.

RIGHT **The long, rough leaves of the large, spreading perennial comfrey (*Symphytum officinale*)**

NAME: **COMFREY**
SYMPHYTUM OFFICINALE
FAMILY: **BORAGINACEAE**

Type: Perennial
USDA zone: Z9–11
Description: Comfrey has a hollow stem and ovate leaves, covered with short stiff hairs that decrease in size as they advance up the stem. It produces drooping clusters of blue-mauve, bell-like flowers.
Height: Up to 3–5ft (1–1.5m) in two years.
Where to grow: Plant in a moist soil in sun or shade. It will also tolerate a clay soil. Comfrey can be found growing in damp places near rivers, but it is decorative enough to be included in the herbaceous border.

How to grow: Comfrey is very easy to grow. Sow the seed in autumn and thin or transplant to 2ft (60cm) apart. Will self-seed if allowed. It can be propagated by root cuttings taken in spring or by division in autumn, which is more effective.

Flowering period: The flowers bloom throughout the summer.

Maintenance: Mulch in spring and autumn for maximum leaf production. Cut down to ground level in autumn, and remove flower stems after flowering. The plant may need containing.

Harvesting and uses: Comfrey has always been used medicinally, and is still widely used in homeopathic medicine. Harvest the leaves as needed. The roots can be dug up in late autumn or winter and used as a poultice. In the past, leaves have been cooked and eaten like spinach. Older leaves can be used to make a liquid fertilizer and for compost.

Pests and problems: Very few. The plant will regenerate from the rootstock and can become invasive and difficult to eradicate.

Other species and varieties: *Symphylum asperum* has bright blue flowers. *Symphytum grandiflorum* is good for ground cover and produces creamy red flowers. *Symphytum officinale* has white and pink flowers borne in late spring/summer.

WARNING: Comfrey should not be taken internally over long periods.

NAME: CORIANDER
CORIANDRUM SATIVUM
FAMILY: UMBELLIFERAE

Type: Half-hardy annual
USDA zone: Z10–11
Description: Coriander is a slender plant that resembles a flat-leaved parsley. It has bright green leaves, fan-shaped at the bottom and wispy at the top, and produces umbels of pinkish-white flowers.
Height: Around 24in (60cm).
Where to grow: Coriander enjoys an open, sunny position and a light, water-retentive soil. Protect from strong winds. Looks best when planted in abundance. It is good in pots and window boxes.
How to grow: Sow seed thinly in shallow drills or in pots under a light covering of fine soil or compost. It takes 5–10 days to germinate, and can be sown in succession between early spring and late autumn. Thin seedlings to 8in

RIGHT **Coriander looks like flat-leaved parsley and produces attractive pinkish-white flowers**

NAME: COTTON LAVENDER
SANTOLINA CHAMAECYPARISSUS
FAMILY: COMPOSITAE

Type: Hardy perennial
USDA zone: Z9–11
Description: Cotton lavender has strongly scented, feathery, silver-grey leaves that are woolly in texture. The silvery, woolly stem is brownish towards the base. It produces lemon-yellow, button-like flowers.
Height: 8–20in (20–50cm).
Where to grow: Cotton lavender enjoys full sun and a fertile, light, well-drained soil, but is happy in most soils. It is good for edging and makes an excellent hedge, and can also be grown indoors.
How to grow: Cotton lavender is not usually grown from seed. It can be propagated from semi-ripe cuttings taken in summer, by root division in spring, or by layering the older stems in summer. Plant 3ft (90cm) apart to allow for growth.
Flowering period: Flowers appear in summer.
Maintenance: Clip the plants in spring to keep them in shape, and again after flowering. Pinch out the growing point to keep them bushy. Deadhead in autumn. Protect if temperatures fall below −5°F (−15°C).
Harvesting and uses: Harvest and dry the leaves before flowering. Cotton lavender is not used medicinally or in cooking, but it makes a good moth repellent.
Pests and problems: None.
Other species and varieties: Italian lavender (*Santolina neapolitana*) has a slightly fruitier scent and longer, more feathery leaves. *Santolina rosmarinifolia* subsp. *canescens* has a less pungent, sweeter scent and small, willow-green leaves.

(20cm) apart to allow for growth when they are large enough to handle. Coriander will produce leaves until the first frosts. It can be grown indoors, but its scent is not pleasant.
Flowering period: Flowers in mid to late autumn, followed by small, round, yellowish brown seeds.
Maintenance: Coriander benefits from regular watering but does not like 'wet feet'. The roots should always be dug up in autumn.
Harvesting and uses: Pick young leaves as required and use in salads or add to curries and stews. To harvest seeds, which have a sweetish flavour, shake from the flower heads. Dry and store whole in airtight jars. Ground seeds are used to flavour chutneys and curries.
Pests and problems: The fine, round stems can become straggly and branching. Like parsley, coriander is difficult to establish.
Other species and varieties: Roman coriander (*Nigella sativa*) is a pungent, aromatic variety. Its seeds are used to flavour bread, chutneys, sauces and curries.
Vietnamese coriander (*Polygonum odoratum*) has a lemon-coriander scent and is often added to meat dishes.

NAME: **COWSLIP**
PRIMULA VERIS
FAMILY: **PRIMULACEAE**

Type: Hardy perennial
USDA zone: Z9–11
Description: The cowslip has slightly crinkled, rosette-forming leaves. The golden-yellow flowers have an orange dot at the base and are borne in long-stalked clusters. The plant has a milky scent.
Height: 6–8in (15–20cm).
Where to grow: Grow in semi-shade or sun in moist, limy, well-drained soil. The cowslip can be grown as an ornamental plant in a rock garden or by the side of a water feature. It is also suitable for indoor cultivation.

How to grow: Pick the seed in early autumn and plant; it will germinate well. Sow seed in autumn under glass. Plant out the following autumn 6in (15cm) apart. Dried seed must have its dormancy broken by first cold then warm temperatures.
Flowering period: The flowers appear in spring. Cowslips are one of the best herbs for attracting bees.
Maintenance: Once established, virtually none, apart from a light dressing of general fertilizer in the spring.
Harvesting and uses: Harvest the flowers as they open and add fresh to salads, candy them, or use for country wine. Roots and flowers can be dried – dried flowers retain their colour well. Use both flowers and roots in pot pourri.
Pests and problems: Vine weevils, virus, leaf miners and root rotting.
Other species and varieties: Primrose *Primula vulgaris* has long, lance-shaped leaves and small, pale yellow flowers with heart-shaped petals. It prefers a moist soil, but has similar uses to the cowslip.

WARNING: May cause allergic reactions or skin rashes.

ABOVE **The cowslip belongs to the same family as the primrose**

NAME: **CREEPING JENNY/MONEYWORT**
LYSIMACHIA NUMMULARIA
FAMILY: **PRIMULACEAE**

Type: Hardy perennial
USDA zone: Z9–11
Description: Creeping Jenny is a mat-forming, moist meadow plant with shiny, heart-shaped leaves growing in opposite pairs, and bell-shaped, yellow flowers borne on stalks.
Height: 3–4in (7.5–10cm).

ABOVE **Creeping Jenny spreads extensively and makes a good ground cover plant.**

Where to grow: Creeping Jenny enjoys light shade, but prefers some sun in cooler climates. It also likes a damp, fertile spot, so is ideal for softening the edges of a pond. Planted outside a pond, it will grow rapidly and trail into the water. It also makes an attractive ground cover plant and grows well in a container, tending to hang down the sides.

How to grow: Can be grown from cuttings and rooted runners. Divided roots can be planted in the spring.

Flowering period: Yellow flowers appear in summer. Generally, no fruit follows, so it does not set seed.

Maintenance: Very little needed, except for regular watering so that the soil stays moist.

Harvesting and uses: Harvest the whole herb in summer to use fresh or dried. It can be used to treat coughs, and the bruised, fresh leaves can be used to treat slowly-healing wounds.

Pests and problems: The herb is considered an invasive weed in a few US states, and it can become a lawn weed if not controlled.

Other species and varieties: *Lysimachia nummularia* 'Aurea' has golden leaves and bears bright yellow flowers in the leaf axils during the summer.

NAME: **CURRY PLANT**
HELICHRYSUM ANGUSTIFOLIUM
FAMILY: **COMPOSITAE**

Type: Moderately hardy
USDA zone: Z8–11
Description: Curry plant has silver foliage with a pepper scent that is strongest after rain, and yellow button-like flowers.
Height: 24in (60cm).
Where to grow: The herb thrives in well-drained soil and a sunny, sheltered position. It provides a silvery edging to formal beds.
How to grow: Seed can be sown under glass in spring. Divide plants in spring, or take semi-ripe cuttings, pot them in a soil-based compost and place them in a cold frame in summer. Plant 12in (30cm) apart in autumn or spring.

ABOVE **Curry plant is an effective insect repellent so it is ideal for planting near the kitchen door**

103

Flowering period: Flowers in late summer.

Maintenance: Prune lightly in early spring or autumn. Protect the roots from frosts in colder areas. Where temperatures plummet, bring the plants indoors for winter.

Harvesting and uses: Harvest the flowers and leaves. Dry petals and use in pot pourri. Dried leaves can be added to soups and casseroles for a mild curry flavour. Add a fresh sprig to stews, rice dishes and pickles. The plant is an effective insect repellent.

Pests and problems: None.

Other species and varieties: *Helichrysum italicum* var. *microphyllum*, is a half-hardy dwarf form just 8in (20cm) high, that is attractive in sink gardens. It also makes a good edging plant.

Helichrysum stoechas 'Goldilocks' is a dwarf shrub with bright yellow flowers.

ABOVE **Dill has a delightful flavour that goes particularly well with fish dishes**

NAME: **DILL**
***ANETHUM GRAVEOLENS* SYN.**
PEUCEDANUM GRAVEOLENS
FAMILY: **UMBELLIFERAE**

Type: Hardy annual

USDA zone: Z9–11

Description: Hollow stem, feathery, very finely divided leaves and umbels of highly aromatic yellow flowers, followed by brown, ridged, aromatic seeds.

Height: 3ft (1m).

Where to grow: Dill likes a light, medium-rich soil with plenty of moisture. It grows well in cool conditions and a sheltered spot, and makes a decorative container plant.

How to grow: Sow seed in spring in shallow drills where it is to grow, in rows 12in (30cm) apart. Thin to 9in (23cm). A second mid-summer sowing will produce a further supply in autumn. Germination usually takes about three weeks, depending on soil temperature. Dill also self-seeds freely, if allowed.

Flowering period: Flowers in mid-summer, followed by the seed.

Maintenance: Support the plants with canes as they grow. Do not allow the soil to dry out.

Harvesting and uses: Harvest leaves just before the plant comes into flower. Collect and dry the seeds after the flower heads turn brown. Both the leaves and flower heads will freeze. Add the flowering tops to pickles, boil the leaves with new potatoes, and use the seeds in soups, bread and fish dishes.

Pests and problems: Runs to seed if it become too dry. Aphids may attack the seed heads.

Other species and varieties: *Anethum graveolens* 'Bouquet' is popular in the US for its seed production. It produces lots of branches and compact flower heads.

Anethum graveolens 'Fernleaf' is an American dwarf cultivar, ideal for containers and slow to bolt. It grows to a height of 18in (45cm) and has dark blue-green foliage.

NAME: **ELECAMPANE**
INULA HELENIUM
FAMILY: **COMPOSITAE**

Type: Hardy perennial

USDA zone: Z9–11

Description: Elecampane is a striking herb with vast 18in (45cm) leaves that are downy on top and smooth underneath, and clusters of yellow, daisy-like flowers. It is a vigorous grower.

Height: 10ft (3m).

Where to grow: Elecampane enjoys a rich, moist, but not waterlogged, soil and full sun. It has great ornamental value, so it should always be put at the back of a border.

How to grow: Seed can be sown in spring. Thin seedlings/plants or transplant to 3–4ft (1–1.2m) apart. The herb can be divided in spring. Offsets taken at this time, with a good root portion and a strong bud, will give almost immediate propagation. It will also self-seed.

Flowering period: Flowers in mid-summer are followed by torpedo-shaped seed.

Maintenance: Stake the plant in summer because it is apt to flop untidily. Cut down the growth in autumn.

Harvesting and uses: Harvest second or third year roots in autumn before they become tough and woody. When sliced, dried and crushed, the root turns from white to grey and smells of violets, ideal for making a fragrant infusion. The root can be crystallized as a sweet, or cooked as a vegetable, though it has a sharp, bitter taste. The root extract is used medicinally, usually for cough relief. Dried petals can be added to pot pourri for colour.

Pests and problems: Mildew is the biggest problem.

Other species and varieties: The normal species only is available.

NAME: **EUCALYPTUS**
EUCALYPTUS GLOBALUS
FAMILY: **MYRTACEAE**

Type: Half-hardy evergreen

USDA zone: Z10–11

Description: Eucalyptus is an evergreen tree with leathery, aromatic bluish-green leaves covered with oil-bearing glands. It bears small, petal-less, white flowers.

Height: 15–50ft (5–17m).

Where to grow: In a well-drained soil and a sunny position protected from cold winds.

How to grow: Sow fresh seed under cover in spring or autumn. Transplant pot-grown plants in spring.

Flowering period: Flowers appear in summer.

Maintenance: Cut back any weak growth in the spring.

Harvesting and uses: Gather leaves at any time. They are an effective flea repellent. The leaves are commercially distilled for their oil or dried for use in medicinal preparations. The timber is used as building material.

Pests and problems: The young leaves are susceptible to frosts.

Other species and varieties: *Eucalyptus citriodora* has attractive leaves which give off a strong lemon scent when rubbed. It can be grown indoors.

Broad-leaved peppermint *Eucalyptus dives*, also known as Australian peppermint, is a short trunked tree with thick foliage when mature that grows to 80ft (25m) high.

River red gum *Eucalyptus camaldulensis* is a spreading riverside tree that grows to 70–150ft (20–45m) in height.

WARNING: Toxic if taken in small doses. Can cause skin irritation.

NAME: **EVENING PRIMROSE**
OENOTHERA BIENNIS
FAMILY: **ONAGRACEAE**

Type: Hardy biennial
USDA zone: Z9–11
Description: Evening primrose has bright green, narrowly elongated leaves and cup-shaped yellow flowers that open in the evening. It grows to a height of 1–5ft (30cm–1.5m).
Where to grow: Enjoys full sun and a light, well-drained soil. It is an attractive plant, good for both borders and the ornamental garden. Not suitable for growing indoors.
How to grow: Sow seed as soon as it is ripe in autumn where the plants are to grow, or in a seedbed for transplanting. The herb usually self-seeds fairly freely once it is established. It can also be propagated by root division or offsets.
Flowering period: The night-scented flowers bloom in summer and are followed by pods containing tiny seeds.
Maintenance: Remove self-seeded seedlings if necessary. Dig up the roots in the second year.
Harvesting and uses: Gather the leaves, flowers and seeds in summer and the roots in early autumn. The ripe seeds are also collected and pressed for oil for commercial use. The herb is used medicinally and as a beauty aid.
Pests and problems: May develop root rot in wet conditions. The leaves can be attacked by downy mildew.
Other species and varieties: Large-flowered evening primrose *Oenothera erythrosepala* has red stems and larger flowers. *Oenothera tetragonal* 'Sundrop' is an attractive variety with reddish, toothed leaves that fade to a delicate, pale and striking dark apricot.

NAME: **FENNEL**
FOENICULUM VULGARE
FAMILY: **UMBELLIFERAE**

Type: Hardy perennial
USDA zone: Z9–11
Description: Fennel has branching stems and finely cut, fern-like leaves. It bears large umbels of yellow flowers.
Height: 6ft 6in (2m).
Where to grow: Prefers a moist, chalky soil in an open, sunny, or slightly shaded position. It is an attractive focal point for a herb border.
How to grow: Sow seed outdoors in spring in drills ¼in (6mm) deep, in rows 18in (45cm) apart, and thin to 18–24in (45–60cm). Fennel self-seeds readily. Water the plants well, and divide the clumps every few years in spring, replanting the side shoots and rooted pieces.
Flowering period: Flowers in late summer.

RIGHT **Fennel's aniseed-flavoured leaves are used in cooking, particularly with fish and poultry**

LEFT Bronze fennel (*Foeniculum vulgare* 'Purpureum') growing in a herb bed

Maintenance: Stake the plants as they grow. Remove any self-seeded seedlings promptly, before the tap roots begin to take hold.

Harvesting and uses: Save the seeds when they are ripe. Dry them, store in an airtight jar and use for aniseed flavouring. Cut whole stalks, tie in bunches and dry. Pick the leaves and stems when tender, and use the sweet aniseed-flavoured leaves in cooking, usually with fish or poultry. Fennel is an important medicinal herb.

Pests and problems: Aphids can infest the seed heads. Plant well away from dill, a close relative, to avoid hybridization.

Other species and varieties: Bronze fennel *Foeniculum vulgare* 'Purpureum' is a slightly hardier, decorative variety that can be planted in the ornamental garden.

Florence fennel *Foeniculum vulgare* var. *dulce* is generally smaller than the other species, growing to a height of 24in (60cm). The bulbous stalk base is used as a vegetable.

NAME: FENUGREEK
TRIGONELLA FOENUM-GRAECUM
FAMILY: LEGUMINOSAE

Type: Half hardy/tender annual
USDA zone: 711

Description: Fennel is an aromatic herb with mid-green, clover-like leaves and pea-like yellowish flowers. It is grown as a spice in most Mediterranean countries.

Height: 24in (60cm).

Where to grow: Feungreek prefers a well-drained, alkaline, fertile soil and a position in the sun. An unusual herb, it is ideal for the middle of the border, though it tends to be untidy. Small plants can be grown indoors.

How to grow: Sow seed thickly in spring where the plants are to grow, in rows 8in (20cm) apart. Thin to 4in (10cm) apart. Sow in succession throughout the summer for young salad leaves.

Flowering period: Solitary or paired, yellowish flowers appear in spring and summer, followed by pods containing yellow-brown seeds.

Maintenance: Feed the seedlings until they are established.

Harvesting and uses: Leaves picked in summer can be used fresh or dried. Dried leaves are used to flavour root vegetables in Indian and Middle Eastern dishes. Collect the seeds when they are ripe, sprout them and use in winter salads. Lightly roasted, ground seeds are an ingredient of curry powder.

Pests and problems: Fenugreek can be difficult to transplant.

Other species and varieties: Normal species only available.

NAME: FEVERFEW
        ***TANACETUM PARTHENIUM* FORMERLY**
        CHRYSANTHEMUM
FAMILY: COMPOSITAE

Type: Hardy perennial
USDA zone: Z9–11
Description: Feverfew is an an attractive herb with finely divided, feathery leaves and masses of white, daisy-like flowers with yellow centres.
Height: 24in (60cm).
Where to grow: In well-drained, light, but moderately rich, soil in full sun.
How to grow: Sow seed in spring in shallow drills where it is to grow. Thin the seedlings to 1ft (30cm) apart. Propagation also by division and by stem cuttings in spring.
Flowering period: The flowers are in bloom from summer until autumn.
Maintenance: Mulch in spring and autumn. Apply a general fertilizer in spring, and cut down growth in autumn. Pot up plants in autumn to overwinter in the greenhouse or conservatory.

ABOVE **Feverfew has attactive feathery leaves and can be overwintered in the conservatory**

Harvesting and uses: The leaves, which are rather bitter, can be used fresh in salads. Chewing one or two freshly-picked leaves can help migraine sufferers, but may cause mouth ulcers. Harvest in summer and dry the whole plant. The leaves can be frozen.
Pests and problems: Generally pest and problem-free.
Other species and varieties: Golden feverfew *Tanacetum parthenium* 'Aureum' is a beautiful, decorative herb that also grows to a height of about 18in (45cm).
Tanacetum parthenium 'Golden Ball' has rounded, golden-yellow flowers.
Tanacetum parthenium 'Golden Moss' is a dwarf cultivar with moss-like, golden foliage, mainly grown for edging and 'carpet bedding'.

ABOVE **Feverfew (*Tanacetum parthenium*) mixed with brightly coloured flowers in the flowerbed**

NAME: FLAX
        LINUM USITATISSIMUM
FAMILY: LINACEAE

Type: Hardy annual
USDA zone: Z9–11
Description: Flax is an erect plant. It has narrow, grey-green leaves and small, single, blue flowers.
Height: 2–4ft (80cm–2m).

Where to grow: Flax prefers a well-drained to dry, sandy soil in a sunny position.

How to grow: Sow seed, which must be kept dry, during spring in drills where the plants are to grow.

Flowering period: Flowers in summer are followed by spherical capsules containing flat, oval brown seeds that are rich in oil.

Maintenance: Must be kept weeded to avoid damage to the roots, which are on the surface.

Harvesting and uses: Mature plants are cut and used for fibre extraction. Ripe seeds are collected and stored whole or pressed for oil, and seed residue is made into linseed cake which is used to feed animals. The whole fresh flowering plant is used medicinally.

Pests and problems: Flax dislikes being transplanted.

Other species and varieties: Purging Flax *Linum catharticum* has oval leaves and white flowers and is used in homeopathic medicine.

ABOVE **Foxgloves have attractive bell-shaped flowers, and provide height as well as colour in the herb garden**

NAME: FOXGLOVE
DIGITALIS PURPUREA
FAMILY: SCROPHULARIACEAE

Type: Hardy biennial
USDA zone: Z9–11
Description: Foxglove is a handsome plant with downy, silvery-grey, pointed leaves. The spikes of bell-shaped flowers vary from purple to rose-colour on the outside but are paler with dark spots inside.

Height: Can grow to 5ft (1.5m)
Where to grow: The foxglove enjoys a moist, acid soil and partial shade. It is popular for both the herb and ornamental garden. Plant groups of plants at the back of the border for eye-catching impact.

How to grow: Sow seed during spring in trays. Plant out in autumn in the flowering position for flowers the following year. Foxgloves will self-seed freely.

Flowering period: The flowers bloom in early summer and are very attractive to bees.

Maintenance: Seeds will spring up all over the garden, which can be a problem. Remove as necessary.

Harvesting and uses: Gather the seed when ripe in late summer for planting the following year. Poisonous herbs, such as the foxglove, are often used medically.

Pests and problems: In damp conditions may develop root rot and crown rot.

Other species and varieties: Woolly foxglove *Digitalis lanata* is a garden variety with fawn-cream flowers, followed by capsules containing a large number of seeds.
Digitalis purpurea 'Alba' is another garden variety with pure white flowers.

WARNING: Foxgloves are poisonous. Do not ingest. Handle with care, and keep them away from children.

NAME: **GARLIC**
ALLIUM SATIVUM
FAMILY: **ULIACEAE**

Type: Hardy perennial
USDA zone: Z9–11
Description: Garlic has grass-like leaves and white flowers, and is usually grown as an annual. The bulb is divided into 8–16 bulblets (cloves), each with a papery white cover.
Height: 1–3ft (30–90cm).
Where to grow: Garlic prefers a fertile, well-drained soil and a sunny site.
How to grow: Plant individual cloves 2in (5cm) deep and 6in (15cm) apart in spring, in rows 12in (30cm) apart.
Flowering period: If allowed to flower, the white flowers will appear in summer.
Maintenance: Keep well watered and weed free until the tops die off in mid- to late summer. If garlic starts to flower during the growing season, nip off the flower bud.
Harvesting and uses: Harvest the bulbs when the tops have died off and the leaves are yellow, and hang in bunches to dry. Garlic improves the flavour of dishes such as pasta, casseroles and stews. Use in salads, dressings and marinades.

ABOVE **Scented-leaf geraniums are grown more for their fragrant leaves than for their flowers.**

Pests and problems: Use a new site every year to avoid attack by white rot. Rust, mildew and onion fly can also be a problem.
Other species and varieties:
Giant garlic or rocambole *Allium scorodoprasum* is a perennial herb with small, milder-flavoured bulbs and pink-purple flowers.

NAME: **GERANIUM – SCENTED-LEAF**
PELARGONIUM **SPP.**
FAMILY: **GERANIACEAE**

Type: Half hardy/tender perennial
USDA zone: Z11
Description: Geraniums have fragrant leaves, usually serrated (depending on variety). Stem round and green, becoming woody with maturity. Insignificant flowers varying from white, violet and mauve to shades of red.
Height: 1–3ft (30cm–1m).
Where to grow: Plant under glass in pots filled with a good quality potting compost. Place in a well-ventilated, sunny position, with plenty of light. Move the plants outside in the warmer summer months.
How to grow: Sow seed (or saved seed) in pots in early spring. Pinch out the growing tips when the plants reach 6in (15cm) high. Tip cuttings can be taken in spring or late summer and potted into individual 3in (7.5cm) pots.
Flowering period: The flowers appear in summer and autumn (depending on variety).
Maintenance: Give a liquid feed with a high potash fertilizer during the growing season. Water when the leaves begin to droop. Cut back one-third of the growth and bring them indoors during winter. Some scented geraniums can grow to gigantic proportions so severe pruning is sometimes necessary.
Harvesting and uses: Pick and dry the leaves just before the flowers open. Dried leaves retain their scent well, and can be added to pot-pourri and herb sachets. Scented geraniums

are grown commercially in various parts of the world for essential oil which is used in aromatherapy, perfumes and toiletries.

Pests and problems: Infestation by aphids and attacks by caterpillars.

Other species and varieties: Peppermint scented geranium *Pelargonium tomentosum* is shrubby and semi-prostrate, with erect stems and peppermint scented leaves.

Pelargonium crispum 'Variegatum' and *P. crispum* 'Prince Rupert' both have lemon-scented foliage. 'Prince Rupert' has greyish leaves with curled edges.

WARNING: Avoid the variety Filicifolium which is slightly poisonous.

NAME: GIPSYWEED (GIPSYWORT)
LYCOPUS EUROPAEUS
FAMILY: LABIATAE

Type: Hardy perennial
USDA zone: Z9–11
Description: Gipsyweed is an erect plant with toothed, narrow leaves and small whorls of tiny, white-pink, bell-shaped flowers around the base of each pair of leaves.
Height: Up to 2–3ft (60–90cm) tall.
Where to grow: Enjoys a moist soil and a position in full sun to partial shade. It is excellent in a bog garden or on the edge of a pond, and attracts insects.
How to grow: Divide established roots and transplant in spring or autumn to the plant's flowering site.
Flowering period: The flowers bloom from early summer until autumn.

ABOVE Nowadays gipsyweed is used medicinally, but it was formerly grown for the black dye it produced

Maintenance: Needs very little maintenance other than keeping the soil moist.
Harvesting and uses: Cut the whole plant down to ground level and dry. In the past, it was used to produce a strong, black dye, but now it is used only medicinally.
Pests and problems: None.
Other species and varieties: Taperleaf water horehound *Lycopus rubellus* 'Moench' is considered a native of the US.
Northern bugleweed *Lycopus uniflorus Michx* is a perennial variety indigenous to the US.

**NAME: GOLDENROD
SOLIDAGO VIRGAUREA**
FAMILY: **COMPOSITAE**

Type: Hardy perennial
USDA zone: Z9–11
Description: Goldenrod has toothed, lanceolate leaves and slender, downy, leafy stems. It bears tiny, bright yellow flowers.
Height: Up to 5ft (1.5m).
Where to grow: Goldenrod enjoys a light soil, in either full sun or in light shade. It is an ornamental plant hat is well suited to the back of the border.
How to grow: Sow seed outdoors in spring. Can be divided in spring or autumn. Occasionally self-seeds.
Flowering period: Flowers in late summer are followed by brown fruits with tufts of short, white hairs.
Maintenance: Lift, divide and replant every three to four years.
Harvesting and uses: Harvest before the flower heads open fully and use fresh or dried. The leaves and flowers yield a yellow dye. Goldenrod is used in homeopathic medicines.
Pests and problems: None.
Other species and varieties: *Solidago* 'Laurin' is a compact perennial bearing spikes of deep yellow flowers in late summer.
Solidago 'Goldenmosa' has yellowish-green leaves and yellow flower heads.
Solidago virgaurea subsp. *minuta* is a mound-forming species with small, lance-shaped, green leaves.

LEFT Goldenrod is a stately plant that is best placed at the back of the herb or mixed border

NAME: **HEARTSEASE (WILD PANSY)** *VIOLA TRICOLOR*
FAMILY: **VIOLACEAE**

Type: Hardy annual/short-lived perennial

USDA zone: Z9–11

Description: The wild pansy of Heartsease has a leafy, spreading stem, oval or lance-shaped leaves and flowers in a combination of purple, lilac, yellow and white.

Height: Up to 15in (38cm).

Where to grow: Prefers a moist, rich, well-drained soil that retains moisture and semi-shade. The small, pretty flowers make it ideal for borders and pots.

How to grow: Sow seed in spring or autumn where the plants are to flower. Press the seed into the soil, but leave uncovered. Also self-seeds readily. Semi-ripe cuttings can be taken in spring and the plants can be divided during the autumn.

Flowering period: The unusual coloured flowers bloom from spring until autumn, and are followed by numerous seed capsules that split into three segments when dry.

Maintenance: Cut back leggy growth to encourage the plants to bush and produce further flowers. Remove dead flower heads to prolong flowering.

Harvesting and uses: Collect and dry whole plants during the flowering season. The plant is used by the pharmaceutical industry, and in the US it is made into an ointment for eczema.

Pests and problems: May be attacked by viral and fungal diseases such as 'pansy sickness'. Slugs and snails can also be a problem.

Other species and varieties: *Viola sororia* syn. *Viola papilionacea* is a North American wild species with purple flowers. In the past, it was used by native Americans to cure headaches and colds.

ABOVE **The wild pansy or heartsease is the plant from which all the colourful varieties of pansy have been developed**

NAME: **HONEYSUCKLE – WILD**
LONICERA PERICLYMENUM
FAMILY: **CAPRIFOLIACEAE**

Type: Hardy evergreen or semi-evergreen
USDA zone: Z9–11
Description: Honeysuckle is a twining climber with oval, glossy leaves and clusters of sweetly scented, pink-cream flowers. In Shakespeare's time, it was known as woodbine.
Height: Can reach 20ft (6m).
How to grow: Sow seeds in pots in autumn. Semi-ripe cuttings can be taken in summer, or hardwood cuttings taken in late autumn.
Where to grow: Honeysuckle likes a good soil and will grow in sun or shade. It looks very attractive when it is trained up walls or twined around pillars.
Flowering period: Flowers in summer are followed by bright red berries.
Maintenance: Prune to remove dead shoots or restrain growth. Mulch with compost in spring. Prune out the flowered wood after flowering.

ABOVE **Honeysuckle is a twining climber that can be trained up walls and will quickly conceal unattractive features**

Harvesting and uses: Harvest the leaves and flowers and dry them. Dig up the roots in autumn for drying. Honeysuckle is recommended for external use only.
Pests and problems: Honeysuckle is prone to attack by aphids and mildew. Seed germination can be slow.
Other species and varieties: Black honeysuckle *Lonicera nigra* bears orange flowers and black berries that are used in homeopathic medicine. Perfoliate honeysuckle *Lonicera caprifolium* is a yellow-flowered species with orange berries.

WARNING: The berries may be poisonous.

NAME: **HOREHOUND**
MARRUBIUM VULGARE
FAMILY: **LABIATAE**

Type: Hardy perennial
USDA zone: Z9–11
Description: Horehound has a hairy, angular stem and grey-green leaves, with deep wrinkles and serrated edges, arranged in pairs. It bears whorls of small, creamy-white flowers.
Height: 24in (60cm).
Where to grow: Enjoys a well-drained, neutral to alkaline soil and a sunny site with protection from cold winds. Can be grown indoors.
How to grow: Sow seed in early spring and thin to 1ft (30cm) apart. Horehound can also be divided in spring or propagated by softwood cuttings in summer.
Flowering period: The flowers, which attract bees, appear in the summer of the second year, followed by shiny, dark brown seeds.
Maintenance: Prune after flowering for a second growth of leaves. Protect the plants from excessive winter wet.

Harvesting and uses: Cut the whole plant when in flower. The flower stems dry well for flower arrangements. The dried leaves can be used to make a medicinal infusion to treat bronchial problems.

Pests and problems: in some parts of the world this herb is controlled as a pest.

Other species and varieties: The normal species only is available.

> **WARNING:** Handling the plants may cause dermatitis. Do not take horehound during pregnancy.

NAME: HORSERADISH
ARMORACIA RUSTICANA
FAMILY: CRUCIFERAE

Type: Hardy perennial
USDA zone: Z9–11
Description: Tall, tap-rooted, pungent plant with large, dark green, scallop-edged, pointed leaves. Small white scented flowers.
Height: 2–3ft (60cm–1m).
Where to grow: Horseradish will grow anywhere, but performs best in full sun and rich soil. It will also thrive in clay soil, but planting in light soil will make it easier to harvest. It is best planted in a corner of the herb garden where it will not disturb other plants.
How to grow: Seed is unobtainable because horseradish is considered sterile. Take root cuttings about 2–3in (5–7cm) long in spring, and plant about 12in (30cm) apart in ground to which organic manure has been added. It can also be increased by division in spring.
Flowering period: Flowers on a tall spike appear in late summer, followed by round seed pods that seldom ripen.
Maintenance: Use a general fertilizer in spring and dig the roots up in autumn.

ABOVE Horseradish will grow anywhere and its roots make a tasty sauce for many different dishes

Harvesting and uses: Lift the roots in autumn and store in a dark, cool place. They can be frozen or grated and preserved in vinegar. Add young leaves to salads. Horseradish sauce is made from the finely grated, thick, white roots, and is very good served with roast beef or fish.

Pests and problems: leaf-attacking insects, mildew and, rarely, clubroot. Invasive and difficult to eradicate completely.

Other species and varieties: *Armoracia rusticana* 'Variegata' is a more attractive variety with bright green basal leaves and a thick, branched tap root.

> **WARNING:** Do not plant near aconite. The roots can easily be confused, with potentially fatal results.

NAME: **HYSSOP**
HYSSOPUS OFFICINALIS
FAMILY: **LABIATAE**

Type: Hardy perennial
USDA zone: Z9–11
Description: Hyssop is an aromatic plant with slim, dark green foliage and spikes of rich blue, occasionally pink or white, flowers.
Height: 2ft (60cm).
Where to grow: Hyssop will tolerate ordinary soil, but prefers one that is light, free-draining and alkaline, and a position in sun or light shade. It makes a good hedge and is ideal for growing in borders. It can also be potted and grown indoors.
How to grow: Sow the seed under glass in early spring, and plant the seedlings out in summer to around 2ft (60cm) apart, or 8in (20cm) apart for hedging. Semi-ripe cuttings can be taken in early summer and the roots divided in spring or autumn.
Flowering period: Flowers bloom in summer.

ABOVE **Hyssop flowers are usually rich blue but may sometimes be pink or white**

Maintenance: Hyssop is a fairly hardy shrub that makes very few demands, but it should be cut back hard in spring and kept well-watered when young.
Harvesting and uses: The leaves can be picked at any time and cooked with a variety of meat dishes. Use only a few because of their strong, slightly bitter taste. The flowers can be gathered and dried and used in hyssop tea. Dried flowers and leaves can be added to pot pourri. The distilled oil is used commercially for liqueurs and to make perfumes.
Pests and problems: None.
Other species and varieties: Rock hyssop *Hyssopus officinalis subsp. aristatus* is a compact cultivar with aromatic leaves and blue-purple flowers. It is an ideal subject for rock gardens and planting between paving stones.

WARNING: Do not take hyssop during pregnancy.

NAME: **JASMINE – COMMON/SUMMER**
JASMINUM OFFICINALE
FAMILY: **OLEACEAE**

Type: Hardy deciduous climber
USDA zone: Z9–11
Description: Jasmine is a deciduous, twining climber that bears fragrant, white flowers. It has green stems and dark green, pinnate leaves.
Height: 30ft (10m).
Where to grow: Jasmine prefers a fertile, well-drained soil and a position in full sun. It can be grown on walls, trellises and pergolas.
How to grow: Sow seeds in spring. Semi-ripe cuttings can be taken in summer. It can also be propagated by layering.
Flowering period: Flowers throughout summer and into autumn are followed by black berries.

Maintenance: The twining, green stems are weak and need to be supported. Jasmine should be cut back after flowering, but not in spring as this will result in lost flowers.

Harvesting and uses: Pick the flowers early in the day before they open. Summer jasmine is used to flavour foods including maraschino cherries. Jasmine petals are used in perfume manufacture. Oil is commercially extracted from the flowers to produce the fragrance for household products such as air-fresheners.

Pests and problems: Plants under cover can be affected by whitefly, aphids, red spider mite and mealy bugs.

Other species and varieties: Winter Jasmine *Jasminum nudiflorum* is popular in gardens. Royal or Spanish Jasmine *Jasminum grandiflora* is an evergreen ramble and a major source of jasmine oil.

Arabian Jasmine *Jasminum sambac* is used in jasmine tea.

> **WARNING:** Jasmine can produce an allergic reaction. Do not take it during pregnancy. The fruit may be toxic.

NAME: JUNIPER
JUNIPERUS COMMUNIS
FAMILY: CUPRESSACEAE

Type: Hardy evergreen
USDA zone: Z9–11
Description: Juniper is a slow-growing, spreading coniferous shrub or tree that bears small, yellow flowers. When mature, it has silvery-green, spiny, needle-like foliage.
Height: 20ft (6m).
Where to grow: In sun or light shade in a good well-drained soil in an open position. It will also tolerate chalky sites and poor soil.
How to grow: Sow seed in a cold frame in spring. Germination may take more than 12 months. When seedlings are about 1in (2.5cm) high, transplant into individual pots, and grow on for two years. Use both male and female plants so the female plants will produce berries, and plant in the same area. Take cuttings in autumn, placing young shoots of the current season's growth in sandy soil in a cold frame. Plant out in spring or autumn.

Flowering period: Flowers in early summer are followed by berries, which in first-year plants are usually green.

Maintenance: Needs little pruning, but can be trimmed into shape if it grows too large.

Harvesting and uses: Berries turn from green to blue-black in the second or third year. Use ripe berries to flavour pork, poultry and especially game. Collect in autumn as soon as they have ripened and dry slowly; they keep well. Juniper berries are used commercially to give gin its distinctive flavour. They can also be added to pot pourri.

Pests and problems: Rust fungus on leaves. Juniper must be cultivated for several years to produce suitable berries.

Other species and varieties: Eastern red cedar *Juniperus virginiana* produces cedar oil for medications and perfume.

Oil of cade (juniper tar) is distilled from the roots of prickly juniper *Juniperus oxycedrus*. 'Nana Ionia' grows to a height of 2ft (60cm), can add interest to window boxes and patios, but does not always bear fruit.

'Hornibrooki' is a wide-spreading prostrate cultivar that grows to just 6in (15cm) high.

> **WARNING:** Juniper berries should not be taken by elderly or very ill people, by anyone with kidney problems, or during early pregnancy. Do not take juniper for longer than three weeks without a break.

NAME: LADY'S BEDSTRAW
GALIUM VERUM
FAMILY: RUBIACEAE

Type: Hardy perennial
USDA zone: Z9–11
Description: Lady's bedstraw is an ornamental plant with numerous, very narrow leaves. The small, bright yellow flowers have a honey scent, and are clustered together on wiry, square, upright stems.
Height: 4ft (1.2m).
Where to grow: Lady's bedstraw enjoys a moist, well drained, neutral to alkaline soil in a shady part of the garden.
How to grow: Sow the seed in late summer, when it has ripened. Use a soil-based compost and leave outdoors to overwinter. The herb can also be propagated by division in the early spring or the autumn.
Flowering period: Flowers mid- to late summer

Maintenance: Little attention required, apart from cutting down the top growth in autumn.
Harvesting and uses: Cut the plants when they are flowering and dry them. They are used to make infusions, tablets and liquid extracts. The stem yields a red dye, and the foliage a yellow dye that is used to colour cheese and butter. _Galium verum_ has been used throughout the years to curdle milk for making cheeses.
Other species and varieties: Woodruff _Galium odoratum_ is a hardy variety with fragrant white, star-shaped flowers that bloom in the summer.
Goosegrass _Galium aparine_ is a scrambling plant with whorls of elliptic leaves and tiny green-white flowers.
Pests and problems: None.

BELOW **The dried flowers of lavender keep their sweet perfume over a long period of time**

NAME: **LAVENDER**
LAVANDULA ANGUSTIFOLIA
FAMILY: **LABIATAE**

Type: Hardy perennial
USDA zone: Z9–11
Description: Lavender has pointed, narrow, grey-green leaves and long spikes of deep mauve flowers. It makes a delightful mass of colour and is ideal for planting as a hedge. It is good grown near the patio, because it will repel insects.
Height: 2–3ft (60–90cm).
Where to grow: Lavenders need full sun, an open position and good drainage. They prefer light, well drained, sandy soil, but will tolerate other soils.
How to grow: Lavender can be grown from seed, which is variable. Sow the seed ¼in (6mm) deep from early spring to early summer, but germination can be erratic and slow. Thin or transplant to 18–24in (45–60cm) apart. It is much better to grow lavender from cuttings. Softwood cuttings should be taken in mid- to late spring from strong sideshoots, and inserted into sandy compost. They are usually slow to root: 6–8 weeks. Heel cuttings can be taken in late summer or early autumn.
Flowering period: Mid- to late summer.
Maintenance: Keep lavender well trimmed to prevent the plants from becoming too woody and straggly. Prune hard after flowering.
Harvesting and uses: Pick lavender as the first flowers open and dry in small bunches. The dried flowers retain their sweet perfume over long periods and can be used in pot pourri and to stuff lavender sachets and pillows. They can also be used in small quantities to flavour cakes, biscuits and confectionery.
Pests and problems: The shoots can become infested by cuckoo spit, which is caused by the larvae of the sap-sucker froghopper insect. Lavender does not like having its roots continually in water.

Other species and varieties: French lavender *Lavandula stoechas* forms an attractive shrub with narrow leaves and tight whorls of small, dark purple flowers with purple tufts that are known as bracts.
Lavandula alba is a white flowering variety.
Lavandula angustifolia 'Lodden Pink' is a traditional favourite with vivid green foliage and lilac pink flowers.
'Munstead' has lavender-blue flowers from early to late summer.
'Hidcote' has deep, rich violet flowers from early summer.

WARNING: Avoid during pregnancy. Do not use if taking insulin for diabetes.

NAME: **LEMON BALM**
MELISSA OFFICINALIS
FAMILY: **LABIATAE**

Type: Hardy perennial
USDA zone: Z9–11
Description: Lemon balm has strong, square stems with branching growth, and deep-veined leaves with a pungent lemon scent. It has insignificant small, pale yellow flowers that grow in clusters.
Height: 12–32in (30–80cm).
Where to grow: Lemon balm likes a fertile, moist soil. It prefers light shade, as full sun can turn the leaves yellow and weaken the scent. The plant is ornamental and makes a useful addition to the border. It is an invasive herb and is suited to growing in a pot.
How to grow: Lemon balm is easily grown from seed sown in spring, although it is slow to germinate. Thin the plants to 2ft (60cm) apart. Lemon balm can also be propagated by

division in the spring or autumn, or by semi-ripe cuttings taken in the summer.

Flowering period: The insignificant, yellow flowers appear in mid- to late summer.

Maintenance: Cut the plants back after they have flowered.

Harvesting and uses: It is best to pick the leaves just before the plant flowers and dry them slowly. The fresh, finely chopped leaves can be added to salads. They also make a wonderfully refreshing tea, and are delicious in long, cool, summer drinks. The dried leaves can be added to pot pourri and used to stuff herb pillows. Lemon balm is one of the main ingredients of the liqueur Chartreuse.

Pests and problems: None.

Other species and varieties: Variegated lemon balm *Melissa officinalis* 'Aurea' has gold-splashed, lemon-scented leaves. *Melissa officinalis* 'All Gold' has attractive golden leaves.

ABOVE **The fresh leaves of lemon balm are delicious in salads and cool summer drinks**

NAME: LEMON VERBENA
ALOYSIA TRIPHYLLA SYN.
LIPPIA CITRIODORA
FAMILY: VERBENACEAE

Type: Half-hardy perennial

USDA zone: Z10–11

Description: Lemon verbena is a graceful shrub with long, tapering, light green leaves and clusters of pinkish-lilac flowers.

Height: 6ft 6in (2m).

Where to grow: The herb prefers a light, well-drained soil. A dry, arid soil will help to keep it sturdy, but planting in a rich, moist loam will result in weak, soft, lush growth. It is easy to cultivate against a sunny garden wall or in a large pot. In cold areas, it can be moved under cover in winter.

How to grow: Dig a planting hole about 12in (30cm) deep in spring and place the plant in it. Keep the roots well watered until it establishes itself. Seed can be difficult to obtain in some countries, so take stem cuttings, which root quickly, in late spring or early summer.

Flowering period: The somewhat insignificant, lemon-scented flowers appear in late summer.

Maintenance: When young shoots appear in early summer, prune the plant lightly to cut out any dead wood and shorten some of the shoots, to maintain a good shape. Prune drooping branches to encourage new growth. In winter, if left outside, cut the herb down and cover the roots with straw or leaf mould.

Harvesting and uses: The aromatic leaves can be used fresh or dried. Harvest in late summer when the plant is at least a year old. Use fresh leaves in oils and dried leaves in pot pourri, sachets and herb pillows.

Pests and problems: Greenfly and hard frosts are the major problems.

Other species and varieties: Normal species only available.

ABOVE **The flowers of lemon verbena are somewhat insignificant, but its aromatic leaves can be used fresh or dried**

How to grow: Sow the fresh seed as soon as it is ripe in late summer, in drills ½in (12mm) deep. Plant out 2ft (60cm) apart during the autumn or spring. Lift the established plants in spring. Replant the side shoots 3ft (1m) apart.
Flowering period: Flowers appear in summer followed by brown, curved, oval fruits.
Maintenance: Tie straw around the stems 2–3 weeks before harvesting for a blanched tender vegetable. Cut the plant back to ground level in the autumn.
Harvesting and uses: Gather the young stems in spring and eat them as a vegetable. The leaves and stems taste like celery, but should be used sparingly because of their strong flavour. The leaves dry and freeze well. Gather the ripe seeds and roots and dry them. Lovage is good added to soups and can also be used in salads. The stems can be candied and the seeds can be added to cream cheese.
Pests and problems: Celery leaf miner.
Other species and varieties: *Levisticum chinensis* is used in Chinese medicine.
Scots lovage *Ligusticum scoticum* has a milder flavour and grows wild on cliffs and seashores.

NAME: LOVAGE
LEVISTICUM OFFICINALE SYN.
LIGUSTICUM LEVISTICUM.
FAMILY: UMBELLIFERAE

Type: Hardy perennial
USDA zone: Z9–11
Description: Lovage has dark green, shiny leaves that grow from hollow stems, and bears umbels of yellow flowers.
Height: 4ft–6ft 6in (1.2–2m).
Where to grow: Lovage will grow more freely in good, deep, rich soil and an open position. It prefers some shade in order to develop its large leaves, and will tolerate stony conditions. It is not suitable for growing indoors. The plant dies back completely in the winter.

NAME: LUNGWORT
PULMONARIA OFFICINALIS
FAMILY: BORAGINACEAE

Type: Hardy perennial
USDA zone: Z9–11
Description: Lungwort has hairy, unbranched stems, a creeping rootstock and oval, pointed, green leaves with silver-white spots. Small, leafy sprays of pink bell-like flowers slowly turn to blue, white or purple as they open fully.
Height: 10–12in (25–30cm).
Where to grow: Lungwort enjoys a light, moist soil and shade or partial shade. A handsome, ornamental plant, it looks attractive planted in clumps at border edges, or as ground cover.

How to grow: Seed should be sown in spring. Germination may take some time, and the best forms do not come true from seed. The plant may also be propagated by division of the roots in spring or autumn.

Flowering period: The bell-like flowers appear in early spring.

Maintenance: The plants should be kept well-watered and mulched in autumn after the foliage has been cut back. The herb should be lifted, divided and replanted every four to five years.

Harvesting and uses: Gather the leaves when young, and harvest the whole plant in early summer. Dry and use for infusions and extracts. Lungwort extract is used commercially as a flavouring ingredient of vermouth.

Pests and problems: The plant can become invasive. The foliage is prone to attack by the larvae of the sawfly.

Other species and varieties: 'Sissinghurst White' *Pulmonaria officinalis* is a very good edging plant. It produces white flowers and grows to a height of 12in (30cm) 'Cambridge Blue' *Pulmonaria officinalis* bears egg-shell-blue flowers that open from pink buds.

WARNING: Lungwort can be a skin irritant and allergen. The herb is subject to legal restrictions in some countries.

NAME: MARIGOLD – POT
CALENDULA OFFICINALIS
FAMILY: COMPOSITAE

Type: Hardy annual
USDA zone: Z9–11
Description: The leaves of pot marigold are pale green, oblong, pointed or blunt-tipped, and slightly hairy. The flowers are usually rich, deep orange but may sometimes be yellow.
Height: 20–28 in (50–70cm).
Where to grow: Pot marigold grows well when it is planted in full sun and a well-drained soil. It does not like heat, so find a cool spot. The flowers will brighten up the dullest corner, so it is ideal for raised beds and pots.
How to grow: Sow the seed 0.5in (12mm) deep in late spring, directly into its growing position. Thin the seedlings to 12in (30cm) apart to allow for spreading. The seed can also be sown under glass in mid-spring and the seedlings transplanted. Sowing seed in late summer will provide plants that will over-winter and flower early the following year. It will also self-seed if some flower heads are left on.

LEFT **The vibrant orange colour of pot marigold**

Flowering period: The flowers bloom throughout the summer until the frosts of autumn. They are at their peak in late summer, attracting bees and other beneficial insects.

Maintenance: Dead-head plants regularly pinch out the top shoots if a short, sturdy plant is required for container growing. Keep the soil moist and give the plants plenty of sunlight.

Harvesting and uses: Pick the flowers when they are open and use them fresh or dried. Infuse them in almond oil to make a soothing hand lotion. Add the petals to fish dishes and salads. The dried petals yield a pale yellow dye and are often used as a substitue for saffron to colour rice. As its name suggests, the herb can also be used in stews. It is also effective as a healing agent: marigold ointment, for example, is good for trreating scratches and grazes.

Pests and problems: The larvae of the sawfly.

Other species and varieties: Hen-and-chickens marigold *Calendula officinalis* 'Prolifera' is grown as a curiosity. The main flower head produces several smaller ones from its base, hence its name.

'Geisha Girl' *Calendula officinalis* is a fast-growing variety that bears heads of double orange flowers.

'Kablouna' *Calendula officinalis* is a bushy annual with lance-shaped, aromatic leaves and daisy-like orange, gold or yellow flowers.

WARNING: Only eat the Calendula officinalis variety. Never eat any member of the Tagetes species, or wild marsh marigolds which are mildly poisonous. Do not drink infusions during pregnancy or when breast-feeding.

ABOVE **Sweet marjoram leaves have an unusual, sweet flavour**

NAME: MARJORAM – SWEET OR KNOTTED
ORIGANUM MAJORANA
FAMILY: LABIATAE

Type: Half-hardy annual.

USDA zone: 10–11

Description: Marjoram is a tender perennial with greyish-green, slightly hairy leaves and small, round, knot-like heads of creamy flowers.

Height: 24in (60cm).

Where to grow: Sweet marjoram dislikes the cold. It prefers a sunny position and a fertile, well-drained, weed-free soil. In temperate climates it is usually treated as a half-hardy annual. It is suitable for container growing.

How to grow: Sow seed under glass in trays and plant the seedlings out 6in (15cm) apart. Seed can also be sown outside in late spring. Cuttings can be taken in early summer and roots can be divided in spring or autumn.

Flowering period: Mid- to late summer.

Maintenance: Seedlings grow very slowly, so good weeding is important. In autumn, cut down plants that will not be brought indoors to 1in (2.5cm) from the ground.

ABOVE **Compact marjoram is ideal for containers, edging and the rock garden. It bears numerous pink-violet flowers**

Harvesting and uses: Marjoram can be used fresh or dried. Harvest the leaves just before the plant flowers, and use to flavour soups, pasta, pizza, and egg and cheese dishes.

Pests and problems: Can be attacked by white fly, aphids and spider mites, especially when brought indoors.

Other species and varieties: Wild marjoram *Origanum vulgare*, known as oregano, has a good, strong flavour and is the easiest of the marjorams to grow.

Pot marjoram *Origanum onites* is a perennial variety that can be grown for winter use, but the flavour is not as good as sweet marjoram. Both wild and pot marjoram depend less on warmth than sweet marjoram, and are therefore easier to grow.

NAME: MINT/SPEARMINT
MENTHA SPICATA
FAMILY: LABIATAE

Type: Hardy perennial
USDA zone: Z10–11
Description: Mint has an erect, square-shaped stem and toothed, bright green, lance-shaped leaves. It bears whorls of pinkish-lilac flowers.
Height: 12–39in (30cm–1m).
Where to grow: Mints enjoy a moist, fertile soil. They prefer partial shade, but will tolerate full sun. They are best sunk into the ground in a bottomless bucket or pot to contain their spreading habit. Mints are also ideal for container planting.
How to grow: Usually raised by root division. It is not advisable to try to grow from seed as the plants do not come true. Take cuttings during the growing season.
Flowering period: Flowers appear in summer and are very attractive to butterflies.

ABOVE **The decorative, woolly leaves of applemint**

ABOVE **Corsican mint has tiny leaves and a creeping habit, so it makes excellent ground cover**

NAME: MULLEIN
VERBASCUM THAPSUS
FAMILY: SCROPHULARIACEAE

Type: Hardy perennial
USDA zone: Z9–11
Description: Mullein is a handsome plant with large, woolly leaves with wavy edges, that form rosettes in the first year and grow up the stem in the second year. It bears tall, closely packed spikes of yellow flowers.
Height: Up to 7ft (2.1m).
Where to grow: Mullein prefers a dry, sunny position, although it will tolerate a wide range of conditions, so it is ideal for the flower border or steep banks.
How to grow: Sow seed in a tray in spring, pressing well into the compost. Transplant the seedlings into small pots when they have their second leaves. Plant in flowering position in early summer, 18in (45cm) apart. It will also self-seed. Take root cuttings in late winter.

Maintenance: Mints need plenty of water and must be kept firmly under control.
Harvesting and uses: Harvest the leaves as required during the growing season and the whole plants as the flowers appear. Mint leaves can be dried or frozen. Chopped fresh mint is particularly good used with lamb and potato dishes. Fresh leaves can be added to oil and vinegar.
Pests and problems: Mint rust.
Other species and varieties: Applemint *Mentha suaveolens* has round woolly leaves and a slight apple fragrance.
Peppermint *Mentha* x *piperita* is good used in summer drinks.
Corsican mint *Mentha requienii* has tiny leaves and flowers and a creeping habit.

RIGHT **Mullein is an ideal plant for the flower border or for growing on steep banks**

Flowering period: Flowers appear from mid-summer to early autumn.

Maintenance: Mullein must be staked if it is planted in rich moist soil or on exposed sites.

Harvesting and uses: Collect the flowers as they open and the leaves during their first season, and dry them. The dried flowers can be added to pot pourri. The herb can also be used for medicinal purposes.

Pests and problems: Mullein is prone to mildew and damage by caterpillars.

Other species and varieties: Large-flowered mullein *Verbascum densiflorum*.
Dark mullein *Verbascum nigrum*.

WARNING: All parts of the herb, except the flowers, are mildly toxic.

NAME: MUSK MALLOW
MALVA MOSCHATA SYN.
HIBISCUS ABELMOCHUS
FAMILY: MALVACEAE

Type: Hardy perennial
USDA zone: Z9–11
Description: Musk mallow has finely-divided leaves and single pink saucer-shaped flowers.
Height: 3–4ft (1–1.2m).
Where to grow: Musk mallow enjoys a rich, free-draining soil in full sun or very light shade. It is an ornamental addition to the herb or flower garden.
How to grow: Sow seed in late spring under glass. In cool climates, musk mallow is grown as a half-hardy annual.
Flowering period: Throughout the summer.
Maintenance: Musk mallow needs staking to keep it tidy, and should be cut back in autumn.
Harvesting and uses: Harvest the leaves and flowers in summer and use them fresh for compresses, and dried for infusions.

Pests and problems: Plants under cover may be attacked by whitefly, and older plants may develop rust.

Other species and varieties: *Malva moschata* 'Alba' bears beautiful white flowers.
Malva neglecta is an almost-prostrate, bushy annual with pink or white flowers, which was widely used by North American Indians.

NAME: MYRTLE
MYRTUS COMMUNIS
FAMILY: MYRTACEAE

Type: Half-hardy evergreen
USDA zone: Z10–11
Description: Myrtle is a slow-growing shrub with dark green, shiny leavesand clusters of sweet-smelling, creamy-white flowers.
Height: Up to 16ft 6in (5m) in its native Mediterranean soil.
Where to grow: Enjoys a position in full sun, protected from the wind, and prefers a well-drained, fertile, acid soil. Myrtle also does well planted in a tub, where it will grow to no more than 2–3ft (60–1m).
How to grow: Sow seed in the greenhouse in spring. Take stem cuttings in mid- or late summer and place under glass. Can also be propagated by layering.
Flowering period: Flowers from mid-summer to autumn, followed by dark blue-black berries.
Maintenance: Do not allow the roots of young plants dry out. Prune the plant to shape after flowering. Protect from frosts during winter.
Harvesting and uses: Gather the buds, flowers and ripe berries as they are available. For the sweetest scent, gather the leaves when the plant is in flower. They can be dried or infused in oil for cosmetic use or in vinegar for culinary uses. Add the dried flowers and leaves to pot pourri. Use the berries to flavour meat and game.

ABOVE **Nasturtium 'Alaska'** (*Tropaeolum majus* 'Alaska') with its creamy-white marbled leaves and yellow flowers

Pests and problems: None.
Other species and varieties: Chilean guava *Myrtis ugni* is a small shrub with rose-pink flowers and mahogany-red fruits which are used in jams.
Myrtus communis subsp. *tarentina* is a more compact variety, ideal for the herb garden.

NAME: NASTURTIUM
TROPAEOLUM MAJUS
FAMILY: TROPAEOLACEAE

Type: Hardy perennial
USDA zone: Z9–11
Description: Nasturtium has creeping or climbing stems, almost-circular leaves and a profusion of long, five-petalled orange, red, cream, or vivid yellow flowers.
Height: Up to 12in (30cm).
Where to grow: Nasturtiums like full sun and do well in a fairly poor, well-drained soil. Rich, over-watered soil will result in a lot of foliage but very few flowers. The plant is good in containers and works well in herbaceous borders. It forms excellent ground cover, and will quickly trail over trellises.
How to grow: Sow the seed in late spring or early summer where the plants are to grow. Seed can also be sown in pots under cover for transplanting after the danger of frosts is over. Nasturtium often self-seeds.
Flowering period: Summer and autumn.
Maintenance: Nasturtiums grow quickly and need to be thinned out regularly.
Harvesting and uses: Gather all parts of the plant in summer. Use the fresh flowers in summer salads or to make nasturtium vinegar. Chop the fresh, peppery leaves and mix with soft cheeses. The seeds can be pickled like capers.
Pests and problems: Nasturtiums are prone to infestations of aphids, and attack by the caterpillars of the large white butterfly.
Other species and varieties: *Tropaeolum majus* 'Double Gleam Mixed' and *Tropaeolum majus* 'Whirlybird Series' have flowers ranging from scarlet and orange to yellow and cream. *Tropaeolum majus* 'Alaska Mixed' has lovely, creamy white, variegated foliage.

NAME: **NETTLE**
URTICA DIOICA
FAMILY: **URTICACEAE**

Type: Hardy perennial
USDA zone: Z9–11
Description: Nettle has pointed, toothed and broadly heart-shaped leaves covered with masses of stinging hairs, and minute greenish flowers. The male flowers grow in spikes and the female flowers hang like curtains on separate plants.
Height: 4ft (1.2m).
Where to grow: In full sun or moderate shade. Will tolerate most soils, but grows best on moist soil, rich in nitrogen. It is ideal for the wildflower garden because it attracts butterflies and provides food for their caterpillars.
How to grow: Sow seed, which can be collected from the wild, in spring. Nettle can also be propagated by root division.
Flowering period: Clusters of flowers in summer and autumn.
Maintenance: Little required, but nettle should be confined because it is so invasive. Lift and divide every autumn, and cut down in summer to provide a second crop of leaves.

Harvesting and uses: Collect the whole plant in summer before it flowers and dry or freeze. Harvest fresh leaves from very young plants and dry for nettle tea. Young leaves and shoots can be eaten as a vegetable (nettle loses its sting when cooked). The young leaf tips can be used to make nettle beer.
Pests and problems: None.
Other species and varieties: Roman nettle *Urtica pilulifera* has similar properties. *Urtica urens* (Annual nettle or burning nettle) is smaller with reddish stems and small, oval, deep green leaves. *Urtica breweri* is a North American species.

> **WARNING:** Handle carefully to avoid the risk of nettle rash.

NAME: **PARSLEY**
PETROSELINUM CRISPUM
FAMILY: **UMBELLIFERAE**

Type: Hardy biennial
USDA zone: Z9–11
Description: Parsley is an attractive herb with bright green, feathery leaves. It produces greenish-white flowers in the second year.
Height: 12–32in (30–80cm).
Where to grow: Parsley likes a fairly rich, non-acid, well-drained soil with plenty of moisture. Some sun is important, but it only grows well when its roots are cool, so it should be shaded for part of the day. It is a good container herb and can be grown on a windowsill.
How to grow: From seed only. Rake soil to a fine tilth and sow seed thinly in spring, and again in late summer for winter use. Sow in rows 18in (45cm) apart and cover lightly with soil. Prick out seedlings, when large enough to handle, to 8in (20cm) apart. Seed can also be sown in small pots. Germination is slow, often

ABOVE **Parsley is one of the most useful herbs, and its vivid green foliage is an attractive sight in any herb garden**

six or seven weeks, but can be helped by soaking the seeds in warm water and pouring boiling water on the soil before sowing.

Flowering period: Flowers appear in flat sprays in early summer. Do not allow to flower or the leaves will be unfit for use and the plant will die after producing seed.

Maintenance: Keep free from weeds and cut out the flowering stems as they appear. Water liberally in dry weather and pick regularly, leaving only the centres of the plants.

Harvesting and uses: Parsley does not dry well but freezes successfully either in large sprigs or chopped into ice cubes. It can be used in hot and cold dishes and as a garnish.

Pests and problems: Parsley is very attractive to slugs, and the larvae of the carrot fly (*Psila rosae*) can affect it. Leaves may also be damaged by leafspot or viral disease.

Other species and varieties: Hamburg parsley *Petroselinum tuberosum* is cultivated mainly for its thick, edible roots.

French/Italian parsley *Petroselinum* var. *neapolitanum* has flat leaves and is similar in taste to *Petroselinum crispum*.

ABOVE **Pennyroyal, one of the mints, is a vigorous grower**

How to grow: Plant 24in (60cm) apart in a border, or 6–8in (15–20cm) apart for a lawn or seat. Sow seed in spring in a seed tray under glass, pressing it well into the compost. Keep moist. Divide roots in spring and autumn and plant 6–9in (15–23cm) apart. Stem cuttings can be taken and will root easily.

Flowering period: Summer to early autumn.

Maintenance: Requires very little attention.

Harvesting and uses: Harvest the whole plant, and use it fresh or dried. It can be used medicinally, to flavour food including Spanish sausages and black puddings, and dried in pot pourri.

Pests and problems: None.

Other species and varieties: Creeping pennyroyal *Mentha pulegium* 'Cunningham Mint' is a fragrant, prostrate variety with an indefinite spread and bright green leaves. It grows to a height of 4–6in (10–15cm).

NAME: PENNYROYAL
   MENTHA PULEGIUM
FAMILY: **LABIATAE**

Type: Hardy perennial
USDA zone: Z9–11
Description: Pennyroyal is an aromatic ground-cover plant with small oval leaves, whorls of lilac flowers and a pungent peppermint scent.
Height: 4–16in (10–40cm).
Where to grow: Pennyroyal enjoys damp shade and moist, light, free-draining soil. It can be used for edging, in a herb ladder or herb seat, or grown in a border. It can also be used as a lawn as it produces a thick mat of growth that suppresses weeds. It is a vigorous grower that spreads very quickly.

WARNING: Do not take in pregnancy as it can induce miscarriage

129

ABOVE **Bright red poppy flower**

The petals can be used dried or fresh, and the seeds whole or ground. Poppy petals will add colour to pot pourri. Whole or ground seeds can be scattered over the top of cakes, bread and biscuits.

Pests and problems: Aphids, powdery mildew and downy mildew.

Other species and varieties: *Papaver rhoas* 'Shirley Single Mixed' is a cultivar that bears pink, rose, white, crimson or salmon flowers. Opium poppy *Papaver somniferum* has crinkled leaves and single stalks of white or mauve flowers. The milky fluid from the unripe seeds is used medically in the drug industry, controlled by international narcotic laws.

WARNING: Immature seeds are toxic. Use only fully-ripe ones.

NAME: POPPY – FIELD
PAPAVER RHOAS
FAMILY: PAPAVERACEAE

Type: Fully-hardy annual
USDA zone: Z7
Description: Poppies have upright stems and long stalks bearing single red flowers with black centres.
Height: 8–36in (20–90cm).
Where to grow: Poppies thrive in a moist, well-drained soil, although they can be found on heavier sites. They look colourful planted in an ornamental border.
How to grow: Sow seed in spring and autumn where the plants are to flower. Poppies do not transplant well. The plant will also self-seed.
Flowering period: Single, red flowers from late spring into autumn, followed by rounded seed capsules. The flowers attract bees.
Maintenance: Remove seed capsules as they appear to stop the plants becoming invasive.
Harvesting and uses: Gather seeds from ripe capsules and the petals as the flowers open.

NAME: PURPLE LOOSESTRIFE
LYTHRUM SALICARIA
FAMILY: LYTHRACEAE

Type: Hardy perennial
USDA zone: Z9–11
Description: Purple loosestrife has square, angled, reddish-brown stems and narrow, pointed leaves. The long, whorled spikes of reddish purple-pink flowers are extremely popular with butterflies.
Height: 5ft (1.5m).
Where to grow: Plant in damp or wet, neutral to alkaline soil in either light shade or full sun. It is ideal for waterside planting.
How to grow: Sow the seed on the surface of moist, compost-filled pots. Leave them to stand in trays of water until the seedlings emerge. The plant can be divided in spring or autumn or new stock grown from basal cuttings in spring. It also self-seeds.

Flowering period: Long spikes of flowers in mid-summer, followed by ovoid seed capsules.

Maintenance: Virtually none, apart from keeping the soil well watered.

Harvesting and uses: Cut the plant while flowering. The whole plant is used fresh or dried in medical preparations.

Pests and problems: Once naturalized it can choke out native plants.

Other species and varieties: *Lythrum salicaria* 'Firecandle' produces slender spikes of rose-red flowers and is ideal for a bog garden.
Lythrum virgatum 'Rose Queen' is a clump-forming perennial that bears four-petalled, light pink flowers from mid to late summer.
Lythrum virgatum 'The Rocket' has slender spikes of rose-red flowers during summer.

NAME: PURSLANE
PORTULACA OLERACEA
FAMILY: PORTULACACEAE

Type: Half-hardy annual
USDA zone: Z10–11
Description: Purslane has fleshy, prostrate, branching stems with thick, dark, spoon-shaped leaves and small yellow flowers.
Height: 8–18in (20–45cm).
Where to grow: Enjoys a moist, rich and well-drained soil in a sunny position.
How to grow: Sow seed in spring where the plant is to flower, and thin the seedlings to 4–6in (10–15cm). It can also be sown in succession at monthly intervals until late summer. Propagation also by root division or cuttings from spring until mid-summer.
Flowering period: The flowers in summer are followed by seed capsules that are filled with tiny black seeds.
Maintenance: Purslane will last longer if the flowers are nipped off when they are in bud, and the plant is cut back after the leaves have been harvested.

Harvesting and uses: Harvest the plants in summer before flowering. Purslane is usually used fresh, and is one of the ingredients of the French soup *Bonne Femme*. Freshly-picked leaves can be added to salads and the shoots can be used as a pot herb. It is also used in oriental cookery.

Pests and problems: Purslane may be attacked by aphids and slugs.

Other species and varieties: Golden purslane *Portulaca oleracea* var. *aurea* is an unusual variety with golden leaves.

ABOVE **Purslane (*Portulaca oleracea*) is an annual with thick, soft trailing stems and small yellow flowers, which appear in summer**

131

NAME: **RAMPION**
CAMPANULA RAPUNCULUS
FAMILY: **CAMPANULACEAE**

Type: Hardy biennial
USDA zone: Z9–11
Description: Rampion has slim, toothed leaves that form a rosette in the first year and a thick, turnip-like taproot. It bears mauve, bell-like flowers in the second season of growth.
Height: 18in–3ft (45–90cm).
Where to grow: Enjoys a light, sandy soil enriched with compost, and a position in full sun. A very decorative plant for the herb garden or border.
How to grow: Usually grown as an annual. Sow seed in spring in a sandy seedbed for a crop of leaves to use in the autumn. Sow in early summer for a winter crop. For root production, sow the seed in a rich soil in a shady position in rows 8in (20cm) apart and thin the seedlings to the same distance. Rampion self-seeds freely. It can also be propagated by root division.
Flowering period: In the second season, the mauve bell-like flowers appear in mid-summer.
Maintenance: Water the plants regularly and earth up in early autumn to blanch the roots. If the herb is to be grown for culinary use, it should not be allowed to flower.
Harvesting and uses: Harvest the leaves, which can be used in salads and as a substitute for spinach, before flowering. Dig the roots in late autumn and store in sand. They can be eaten cooked or raw.
Pests and problems: The plant will sometimes go to seed in a hot summer.
Other species and varieties: *Campanula persicifolia* is a favourite in the herb border and grows to a height of 3ft (1m). *Campanula rapunculoides* var. *ucranica* has smooth-textured foliage and violet/lavender flowers.

NAME: **ROCKET**
ERUCA VESICARIA SUBSP. *SATIVA*
FAMILY: **CRUCIFERAE**

Type: Hardy annual
USDA zone: Z9–11
Description: Rocket is a fast-growing herb with indented, dark green leaves, branched leafy main stems, and sparse four-petalled creamy-white flowers.
Height: 2–3ft (60cm–1m).
Where to grow: Rocket enjoys a sunny position but it will also do well in partial shade. It will tolerate most types of soil, but does best in one that is moist, rich and preferably alkaline.
How to grow: Sow seed in succession from early spring to early summer where the plants are to grow. Thin to 12in (30cm) apart. Grow the early spring sowings under cloches. The plant often self-seeds, and can also be propagated by division.
Flowering period: Flowers appear from late winter to autumn, followed by seed pods.

ABOVE Fresh rocket leaves have a distinctive flavour and are a popular addition to salads

Maintenance: Keep well watered in dry weather to prevent the plants from bolting. Cut old growth back in spring.

Harvesting and uses: Harvest the leaves before the flowers appear as those picked later have a coarser flavour.

Pests and problems: Flea beetles can attack and damage the leaves. May also be affected by clubroot and mildew.

Other species and varieties: The normal species is the one most usually cultivated.

NAME: ROSE
ROSA GALLICA* VAR. *OFFICINALIS
FAMILY: ROSACEAE

Type: Perennial
USDA zone: Z9–11
Description: Roses are bushy, deciduous shrubs with strong, upright stems, dull green, leathery, divided leaves and fragrant, crimson flowers.
Height: 32in (80cm).
Where to grow: The rose enjoys a well-drained, moist, fertile soil and a sunny position.

ABOVE **There are many different varieties of rose, including this white Rugosa rose with its dark green divided leaves**

ABOVE **The dog rose adds colour to any garden**

They can be grown as a shrub suitable for the herb garden or ornamental border. Roses may also be planted as a hedge.

How to grow: Plant during the dormant season in deeply dug soil with manure or well-rotted compost added. Make sure the planting hole is large enough to accommodate the roots or rootballs, and allow around 2ft 6in–4ft (75–120cm) between each plant. Can be propagated by budding in summer and hardwood cuttings in autumn.

Flowering period: The flowers bloom in summer, and are followed by brick-red hips during the autumn.

Maintenance: Mulch the plants in spring and apply a liquid feed in summer. Prune in spring, cutting away any dead growth and suckers. Remove dead flowers and any dead leaves as soon as possible. Roses should be watered frequently. Gently clip over any *gallica* roses used for hedging.

Harvesting and uses: Pick the roses in summer, and crystallize the fresh petals or use to make rose petal honey or rose petal sugar. Dried leaves will add fragrance to pot pourri, herb sachets, and herb cushions. Pick rosehips in autumn and use to make rosehip syrup.

ABOVE The flowers of roses are followed by bright red hips that add autumn colour to the garden

Pests and problems: Aphids, mildew, blackspot, rust and sawfly.

Other species and varieties: *Rosa eglanteria* (Sweet briar/eglantine) is a deciduous shrub with hooked thorns, apple-scented leaves and sweetly perfumed, bright pink flowers that appear in summer.

Rosa rugosa has very prickly stems, dark green leaves and scented white or purple-pink flowers. Dog rose *Rosa canina* has single pink or white flowers.

NAME: **ROSEMARY** *ROSMARINUS OFFICINALIS*
FAMILY: **LABIATAE**

Type: Hardy perennial
USDA zone: Z9–11
Description: Rosemary has long, spiky leaves, green above and whitish beneath, and a pungent, aromatic scent. It bears small, pale blue flowers. Once it has reached its maximum height, it will start to grow sideways.
Height: Up to 6ft 6in (2m).
Where to grow: Rosemary thrives in a light, sandy, well-drained soil and a sunny, sheltered position. It grows well against a wall. It can also be grown in a large pot, and is an ideal subject for the conservatory, rarely growing over 3ft (1m) when potted.
How to grow: Rosemary is difficult to cultivate from seed, but try sowing in trays under glass in mid- to late spring to produce decent plants by autumn. It is more commonly raised from cuttings taken from the top of branches or side

ABOVE Rosemary will grow into a large shrub, but must be cut back to prevent it becoming straggly

shoots from early spring to early autumn. The strong, rooted cuttings can be overwintered in the greenhouse to form good plants by the second year. Pinch out the tops of cuttings when transplanting to encourage bushiness.

Flowering period: Small, pale blue flowers start to appear in clusters in late winter if the weather is mild, and continue until late spring. Rosemary is a useful bee plant.

Maintenance: Minimal. Cut back growth after flowering to prevent it from becoming straggly and woody. Do not cut into the old wood or the plant will die.

Harvesting and uses: Pick only as needed. Leaves can be gathered for immediate use or for drying at any time. Dried leaves retain their flavour well. Harvest sprigs to use in strong dishes, stews, roasts, sauces and stuffings.

Pests and problems: Rosemary is hardy except in severe weather conditions and wet soil. Cold, frosty weather can destroy it completely.

Other species and varieties: *Rosmarinus officinalis* 'Miss Jessopp's Upright' has pale blue flowers and lighter, brighter leaves, and is useful for hedging.

Rosmarinus officinalis var. *albiflorus* has white-flowers and is excellent for flower arranging.

Rosmarinus officinalis 'Fota Blue' is a rather tender, semi-prostrate variety which bears dark blue flowers.

NAME: RUE
RUTA GRAVEOLENS
FAMILY: RUTACEAE

Type: Hardy perennial
USDA zone: Z9–11
Description: Rue has distinctive green-blue, finely-cut, aromatic leaves and umbels of small, soft yellow flowers.
Height: Up to 24in (60cm).
Where to grow: Prefers a well-drained soil with a little lime and a position in full sun, but will grow almost anywhere. It is extremely decorative in the herb garden.

How to grow: Sow seed in mid-spring, and transplant the seedlings at a distance of about 12in (30cm) apart. Can be propagated by stem cuttings in late spring and summer, and also by root division. Will self-seed if permitted.

Flowering period: The umbels of small, soft yellow flowers appear in summer.

Maintenance: Prune the plants in spring to encourage bushy growth.

Harvesting and uses: Harvest the leaves from the flowering plants and use fresh or dried. Rue is widely used by herbalists.

Pests and problems: None.

Other species and varieties: *Ruta graveolens* 'Jackman's Blue' has much bluer leaves and is very aromatic.

Ruta graveolens 'Variegata' is one of the few variegated cultivars that comes true from seed.

WARNING: Wear gloves when handling rue as it can irritate the skin. In large quantities, the leaves can be poisonous.

ABOVE Rue (*Ruta graveolens*) growing in the herb garden

135

ABOVE **Sage is a bushy, wide-spreading evergreen with pretty mauve-blue flowers**

NAME: SAGE
   SALVIA OFFICINALIS
FAMILY: LABIATAE

Type: Hardy evergreen
USDA zone: Z9–11
Description: Sage is a bushy, wide-spreading hardy evergreen with grey-green leaves and mauve-blue flowers.
Height: 24–32in (60–80cm).
Where to grow: Sage enjoys a dry, sunny spot, sheltered from cold wind, and prefers a light, well-drained, slightly chalky soil.
How to grow: Plant 18–24in (45–60cm) apart in the prepared site, allowing 24in (60cm) all round. Place a light, firm stake that will be at the centre of the bush when it grows. Pinch out the growing tip soon after planting. Once established, it will produce new branches every year. Sage is easily grown from seed. Sow in ½in (12mm) deep drills in the spring and thin the seedlings to 8–9in (20–23cm) apart. Germination will take about two weeks. Transplant to a permanent position

the following spring. Cuttings can be taken from early spring to early autumn, and will root quickly if given some bottom heat. Take them with a 'heel' and plant in an open, sunny position. Sage can also be propagated by layering, and the side shoots root in about eight weeks. Choose a different place for fresh plants as sage does not do well when replanted in the same soil.
Flowering period: Spikes of flowers ½in (12mm) long appear in summer.
Maintenance: Pinch out the growing tip once the plant is established. As the bush grows, tie the main stem to the stake. Prune back in autumn after flowering. Two or three-year-old bushes tend to become straggly, so remove any new branches to make new plants.
Harvesting and uses: Pick leaves for drying before the plant begins to flower. The leaves also freeze well. Use in stuffings with pork and chicken. Make sage butter and sage vinegar.
Pests and problems: Small green caterpillars may eat the leaves. The leaves may turn yellow

if the roots need more space. Roots may rot if the plant is overwatered.

Other species and varieties: Jerusalem sage *Phlomis fruticosa* has silvery-green, wrinkled, wedge-shaped leaves covered with woolly, yellow hairs. It is used mainly as an ornamental shrub and will grow to 10ft (3m).

Golden sage *Salvia officinalis* 'Icterina' is a golden-leaved variety with a milder flavour than common sage.

Red sage *Salvia officinalis* 'Purpurascens' is a handsome variety with strongly-flavoured leaves. Clary sage *Salvia sclarea* is a biennial herb with long-lasting lilac flowers.

NAME: **ST JOHN'S WORT**
HYPERICUM PERFORATUM
FAMILY: **HYPERICACEAE**

Type: Hardy perennial
USDA zone: 79–11
Description: St John's wort is a rather sprawling plant with small, pale green, elongated leaves. It bears star-like, bright yellow flowers.
Height: 12–24in (30–60cm) after 2–3 years.
Where to grow: Enjoys a sunny or partly shaded position. Will tolerate most soils, but prefers one that is well-drained or dry.
How to grow: Sow seed in spring in seed trays under cover. Stem cuttings can be taken in spring before the herb flowers, and the roots divided in spring or autumn.
Flowering period: The bright yellow flowers bloom from mid- to late summer.
Maintenance: Damaged stems should be pruned after the frosts are over.
Harvesting and uses: Harvest the plants just as they are flowering and use fresh or dried in infusions, oils and liquid extracts. The herb has been used medicinally for centuries and is still used extensively in homeopathic medicine.
Pests and problems: None.

Other species and varieties: All-heal *Hypericum androsaemum* is a larger, shade-loving plant with oval leaves and black berries in autumn.

WARNING: St John's wort may cause dermatitis, especially on skin exposed to direct sunlight. The raw plant can be harmful if it is eaten.

NAME: **SALAD BURNET**
SANGUISORBA MINOR
FAMILY: **ROSACEAE**

Type: Hardy perennial
USDA zone: 79–11
Description: Salad burnet is a decorative, hardy plant with a dense rosette of leaves from which stems of small toothed, green leaves spray out. It has red-dotted, round heads of tiny green flowers.
Height: 30in (75cm).

ABOVE Salad burnet is a very decorative herb with lacy, cucumber-scented foliage

How to grow: Salad burnet is easily grown from seed sown in mid-spring. Thin out the seedlings to 12in (30cm) apart. It will also self-seed if permitted. Established plants can be propagated by division in early spring.

Where to grow: Salad burnet enjoys an open, sunny position and will thrive in most soils, but it does well on fertile, chalky ones. It can be planted as an edging to formal gardens.

Flowering period: The heads of tiny green flowers bloom throughout the summer.

Maintenance: Cut the flower heads to ensure a good supply of fresh leaves and to prevent it from self-seeding. Water well in dry weather.

Harvesting and uses: The young foliage, which is cucumber scented and lace-like in appearance, can be picked as required and can also be dried. Use in herb butters, soft cheeses, salads and casseroles.

Pests and problems: Relatively problem-free.

Other species and varieties: Great burnet *Sanguisorba officinalis* is taller with deep red, rectangular flower heads. It has similar uses.

NAME: SELFHEAL
PRUNELLA VULGARIS
FAMILY: LABIATAE

Type: Hardy perennial
USDA zone: Z9–11
Description: Deep purple, pink or white flower heads in dense whorls on square stalks. A creeping rhizome and long, narrow, bright green, pointed and toothed leaves.
Height: 12in (30cm).
Where to grow: Selfheal prefers moist, well-drained soil in light shade or sun. It can be used as ground cover in the herb garden or border, and is also suited to the rock garden. Growing it in grass will help to restrain any unnatural growth.
How to grow: Sow the seed out of doors in autumn or spring. Selfheal can also be

propagated by cuttings, or by dividing roots in spring and planting out 8in (20cm) apart.

Flowering period: The flowers appear in mid-summer and are very attractive to butterflies.

Maintenance: Water regularly, but do not overwater. Control the plants if they start to become invasive.

Harvesting and uses: Harvest the flowering plant and use fresh or dried. The herb is used medicinally for mouth ulcers, sore throats and in infusions and ointments.

Pests and problems: The plants are much larger when grown in fertile soil and can become invasive.

Other species and varieties: Large selfheal *Prunella grandiflora* is a semi-evergreen variety with whorls of purple flowers that bloom in summer. Prunella bears short spikes of funnel-shaped purple flowers in mid-summer.

NAME: SORREL
RUMEX ACETOSA
FAMILY: POLYGONACEAE

Type: Half-hardy annual
USDA zone: Z10–11
Description: Sorrel has wide, arrow-shaped leaves and tall stems clustered with small, rust-red flowers.
Height: 3ft (1m).
Where to grow: The herb prefers a moist, fertile soil and a position in sun or partial shade. It is good in the herb garden although, once established, it can spread like a weed and become a nuisance.
How to grow: Sow seed in spring where the plants are to grow. Thin out the seedlings to about 12in (30cm) apart. The plants can also be divided in autumn.
Flowering period: Flowers appear in summer and tiny fruits follow shortly afterwards.
Maintenance: Remove the flower buds to maintain a good supply of young, tender

ABOVE **Young sorrel leaves can be snipped over salads or used to add flavour to omelettes**

leaves. Pots of sorrel can be kept under glass to ensure a winter supply.

Harvesting and uses: Harvest the young leaves before the plant flowers and use them fresh. The leaves can be snipped over salads or added to omelettes. They also puree well, and can be frozen for later use.

Pests and problems: Fungal leaf spots. Prone to attack by leaf-eating insects.

Other species and varieties: French sorrel *Rumex scutatus* has spear-shaped leaves and red-green flowers that turn pale brown as the fruits ripen.

Rumex scutatus 'Silver Shield' is a cultivar that makes a good ground cover plant, particularly at the front of borders.

RIGHT **Southernwood (*Artemisia abrotanum*) is a semi-evergreen shrub with grey-green leaves**

NAME: **SOUTHERNWOOD**
ARTEMISIA ABROTANUM
FAMILY: **COMPOSITAE**

Type: Hardy perennial
USDA zone: Z9–11
Description: Southernwood is a small perennial shrub that produces long, woody stems. It has downy, feathery, grey-green leaves and an aromatic perfume rather like camphor. It has small, yellow-white flowers.
Height: 4ft (1.2m).
Where to grow: Southernwood prefers a well-drained soil in a sunny position. It is highly ornamental, so it is an ideal subject for the herb garden where its finely toothed foliage is a foil for more colourful plants. It can also be grown as an informal hedge.
How to grow: Seed is not available. Softwood cuttings taken in spring will root easily. Plant out 15in (38cm) apart. Heel cuttings can be taken in autumn.

Flowering period: The flowers appear in late summer, but the herb may not produce flowers in cooler climates.

Maintenance: To promote the growth of foliage, cut back to two buds of the previous year's growth in spring.

Harvesting and uses: Harvest and dry the leaves in summer. They can be used in sachets to deter moths.

Pests and problems: Cuckoo spit caused by the larvae of the sap-sucker froghopper insect.

Other species and varieties: Wormwood (see separate listing) is a sub-shrub with grey-green foliage and insignificant, yellow flowers that grows to a height of 3ft (1m).

Fragrant wormwood *Artemisia capillaris* is an aromatic subshrub with silky leaves and purple-brown flowers that bloom from late summer.

NAME: STRAWBERRY – WILD
FRAGARIA VESCA
FAMILY: ROSACEAE

Type: Hardy perennial
USDA zone: Z9–11
Description: The wild strawberry has a ridged, hairy, reddish green stem with bright green, three-lobed toothed leaves and dainty, white, yellow-centred flowers.
Height: Around 10in (25cm).
Where to grow: Wild strawberries prefer light, free-draining, alkaline soil in light shade. They can be planted in a strawberry bed or as an edging in the herb garden, and make good ground cover.
How to grow: Wild strawberries can be raised from seed, but are best obtained as plants. In a bed, space at 12in (30cm) each way. Can be propagated from the long, self-rooting runners produced from the stem area.
Flowering period: Flowers from early spring until the first frosts of autumn, followed by bright red fruits with seeds embedded in the skin.

Maintenance: The plants can be given a light dressing of fertilizer in spring. Net to protect the fruit from birds. Trim the foliage to about 2in (5–6cm) after fruiting. Strawberry plants will deteriorate over a period of time so should be replaced.

Harvesting and uses: Pick the ripe fruit in summer and eat fresh, freeze or bottle. Collect the leaves in early summer and the roots in autumn, and dry for use in decoctions and infusions, or add to pot pourri.

Pests and problems: Slugs and mildew.

Other species and varieties: Musk strawberry *Fragaria moschata* is also a wild species but with larger flowers.

Fragaria virginiana is a red-fruited wild species that was very important medicinally to the North American Indians.

WARNING: Some people are allergic to strawberries.

NAME: SUMMER SAVORY
SATUREJA HORTENSIS
FAMILY: LABIATAE

Type: Moderately-hardy annual
USDA zone: Z10–11
Description: Summer savory is an aromatic herb with straggly, tough or erect stems, long, leathery, pointed, dark green leaves, and white or pink flowers produced in small spikes.
Height: Up to 15in (38cm).
Where to grow: Grows well in a rich, light soil and an open, sunny position. Good container herb.
How to grow: Sow seed in spring in shallow drills 9–12in (23–30cm) apart. Thin the seedlings, which are slow to germinate, to 6in (15cm) apart.
Flowering period: Flowers in late summer.

Maintenance: Pinch out the tops to prevent the plants from growing leggy. Cut back in early spring to encourage new growth.

Harvesting and uses: Leaves can be used fresh or dried, and should be gathered before the plant flowers. Freezes well and keeps its flavour. Use sparingly in meat dishes and stuffings and with cabbage, beans and peas.

Pests and problems: Virtually problem-free.

Other species and varieties: Winter savory *Satureja montana* is a related perennial with a stronger flavour than summer savory (see separate listing).

Creeping winter savory *Satureja spicigera* (*S. repanda*) has strongly flavoured, deep green leaves and bears tiny white flowers. It is a good container herb and will also grow well on a windowsill.

ABOVE **A bee visiting a big yellow sunflower (*Helianthus annuus*)**

| NAME: **SUNFLOWER** |
| *HELIANTHUS ANNUUS* |
| FAMILY: **COMPOSITAE** |

Type: Hardy annual

USDA zone: Z10–11

Description: The sunflower is an impressive, ornamental plant with a tall, thick, light green stem and heart-shaped, toothed leaves. The stem is topped by a massive, daisy-like, golden yellow flower, with a purple-brown central disc of tube florets.

Height: 10ft (3m) or more.

Where to grow: The sunflower enjoys a rich, free-draining soil in full sun with shelter from the wind. It is not suitable for growing indoors.

How to grow: Best raised as a half-hardy annual. Sow seed where it is to flower. Seedlings should be thinned to 12–18in (30–45cm) apart.

Flowering period: Begins in late summer and continues until the first frosts of autumn.

Maintenance: The stalks should be supported with stout canes before the flowers start to appear. Sunflowers need regular watering.

Harvesting and uses: Harvest and dry both the leaves and seeds. Flower heads should be collected when they droop and hung until the seeds fall. Seeds can be shelled and the kernels eaten fresh or roasted, or added to bread. Sprouted seeds can be added to sandwiches and salads. Sunflower oil is extracted commercially from the seeds. Birds love to eat the hulled seeds, which are known as sunflower hearts.

Pests and problems: Mildew is possible although it does not usually occur until after flowering. The plant can also be troubled by insect pests. It is best not to plant the herb near a potato plot as its growth could be stunted.

Other species and varieties: *Helianthus annuus* 'Lemon Queen' has pale yellow daisy-like flowers, grows to a height of 6ft (1.8m) and is an ideal plant for the back of a border. *Helianthus annuus* 'Teddy Bear' is a dwarf cultivar of the genus.

ABOVE Sweet violet has glossy heart-shaped leaves and delicate flowers

NAME: **SWEET CICELY**
MYRRHIS ODORATA
FAMILY: **UMBELLIFERAE**

Type: Hardy perennial
USDA zone: Z9–11
Description: Sweet cicely has hollow stems with long, downy fern-like leaves and loose umbels of tiny, white flowers.
Height: 3–6ft (1–2m).
Where to grow: Sweet cicely prefers a fertile, moist, cool soil and partial shade, although it will tolerate sun. It is valued as an ornamental herb and is well suited to growing in a shady corner of the herb garden.
How to grow: Sow seed under glass in late spring in a soil-based compost. Will self-seed given the right conditions. Propagation also by root division in autumn or spring.
Flowering period: Flowers appear from late spring, followed by clusters of ridged fruits.
Maintenance: Cut back growth as soon as the foliage dies down in late autumn.
Harvesting and uses: Pick the leaves during the growing season and used fresh or frozen.

Collect the seeds and use them fresh. All parts of the plant have a sweetish taste with a hint of aniseed, but the leaves are the part to use. The herb is a natural sweetener and can be stewed with fruit such as gooseberries to counteract their acidity. It can be used in summer puddings, jellies, mousses and fruit salads.
Pests and problems: Prone to mildew.
Other species and varieties: Normal species only available.

NAME: **SWEET VIOLET**
VIOLA ODORATA
FAMILY: **VIOLACEAE**

Type: Hardy perennial
USDA zone: Z9–11
Description: Sweet violet is a highly-scented, spreading plant with heart-shaped, mid- to dark green leaves. It bears delicate flowers that are violet or white.
Height: 4–6in (10–15cm).
Where to grow: Sweet violet will grow in

poor soil as long as it is moist, though a rich, moist soil is better. It prefers light to moderate shade. It makes an excellent ground cover plant and can be planted at the front of borders. It is not suitable for growing indoors.

How to grow: Seed can be sown in spring or autumn, but germination is erratic. It is much easier to increase the herb from rooted runners or by root division. Transplant rooted runners in early spring, leaving 4–5in (10–12.5cm) between each plant.

Flowering period: The perfumed flowers appear from late winter to mid-spring.

Maintenance: Virtually none once the plant is established, apart from regular dead heading.

Harvesting and uses: The leaves should be gathered in early spring, the flowers when they first open, and the roots in autumn. The flowers can be crystallized or eaten raw in salads. Dried flowers can be used in pot pourri. An infusion of the root is said to ease catarrh.

Pests and problems: Sweet violet can be prone to fungal diseases. It may also be damaged by slugs and snails.

Other species and varieties: *Viola odorata* 'Alba' bears a profusion of white flowers and is the most widely grown cultivar.

> **WARNING:** Violets contain saponins that may cause nausea.

NAME: TANSY
**   *TANACETUM VULGARE***
FAMILY: COMPOSITAE

Type: Hardy perennial

USDA zone: Z9–11

Description: Tansy is a fragrant herb with dark green leaves made up of toothed leaflets and flat umbels of golden-yellow, button-like flowers.

Height: 2–4ft (60cm–1.2m).

How to grow: Sow seed in spring ½in (1.5cm) deep. Tansy self-seeds freely. It can also be propagated by root division in autumn, by taking basal cuttings in spring, and by semi-ripe cuttings in the summer.

Where to grow: Tansy prefers a moist, well-drained soil but will grow happily in most soil

RIGHT **Tansy (*Tanacetum vulgare*) is a very aromatic herb with decorative fern-like leaves and yellow button flowers**

143

types. It is an attractive border plant.

Flowering period: The flowers bloom from mid- to late summer.

Maintenance: Tansy is very invasive, but can be contained by chopping round the clump and pulling out unwanted roots. Dead-head regularly. Cut dead stems back in winter.

Harvesting and uses: Harvest the leaves in spring and summer and dried. The flowers should be cut just before their peak and dried. Tansy leaves yield a yellow dye, but nowadays the plant is used mostly by herbalists.

Pests and problems: None.

Other species and varieties: Fern-leaved tansy *Tanacetum vulgare var. crispum* has beautifully cut leaves but is more compact and less pungently scented.

Tanacetum vulgare 'Isla Gold' is extremely ornamental with golden foliage, and enjoys a position in full sun.

WARNING: Tansy should not be used during pregnancy.

ABOVE **Tarragon leaves have a strong, aniseed flavour and can be used in salads, stuffings and sauces**

NAME: TARRAGON (FRENCH)
ARTEMISIA DRACUNCULUS
FAMILY: COMPOSITAE

Type: Moderately-hardy perennial

USDA zone: Z10–11

Description: Tarragon has long, thin, green leaves. Its flowers are woolly and greyish-green or white in colour.

Height: 18–39in (45cm–1m).

Where to grow: Tarragon grows best in warm, fairly dry conditions. The soil should be well-drained, light and fairly poor, and either sandy or stony.

How to grow: Plant in early spring and autumn, leaving 24in (60cm) between each plant. Tarragon cannot be propagated from seed. Divide roots or take cuttings in spring.

Flowering period: Insignificant flowers, which rarely open, in late summer.

Maintenance: Remove flower shoots to encourage leaf growth, and trim regularly to promote a stronger flavour. Do not add fertilizer to the soil as it will encourage tall, straggly growth. Divide and replant in fresh soil every four years. Cover the roots with straw or leaf mould when severe frosts are expected.

Harvesting and uses: Leaves can be picked in summer and chopped into salads, stuffings and sauces. They also dry and freeze well. Has a strong aniseed flavour so use sparingly.

Pests and problems: Avoid cold, wet soil.

Other species and varieties: Russian tarragon *Artemisia dracunculoides* looks similar, but has coarser, almost tasteless leaves.

NAME: THYME
THYMUS VULGARIS
FAMILY: LABIATAE

Type: Perennial
USDA zone: Z9–11
Description: Thyme is an evergreen perennial with small, round, greyish-green, highly aromatic leaves and small, starry, pale mauve flowers. The flowers of all varieties of thyme are attractive to butterflies and bees.
Height: Up to 18in (45cm).
Where to grow: Thyme will thrive in dry conditions and poorish soil. It needs protection from wind and enjoys a sheltered corner. It is good for rock gardens, patios, for softening edges of paving stones and to decorate pots of herbs by creeping out of holes and crevices. It can be grown indoors for frequent cutting for culinary use.
How to grow: Sow seed where it is to grow. Thin seedlings to 12–18in (30–45cm) apart, or sow in trays and transplant the seedlings. Buy young plants and set out in mid to late spring. Take cuttings with a heel attached in summer and root in pots of sandy soil in an outside frame or on a sunny windowsill. Thyme can also be propagated by mound layering.
Flowering period: Flowers in summer.

ABOVE **Thymus vulgaris 'Silver Posie' has a lovely scent**

Maintenance: Cut out older wood to encourage new shoots. Trim back faded flowers. For the best flavour, clip in spring to prevent flowering, or clip immediately after blooming to stop it becoming straggly. Protect during winter in cold, wet areas.
Harvesting and uses: Thyme can be dried, but does not freeze well. It is delicious with eggs, in casseroles, soups and cheese sauces, and is a basic ingredient of bouquet garni.
Pests and problems: Very few.
Other species and varieties: Lemon thyme *Thymus citriodorus* has a strong lemon scent. *Thymus vulgaris* 'Silver Posie' has a truly wonderful smell.
Thyme 'Doone Valley' gives off a lovely perfume. Thyme 'Ruby Glow' has a creeping habit and is ideal for growing in herb rockeries, containers, and for growing in crevices in paths.

LEFT **Thyme 'Ruby Glow' is a creeping thyme with aromatic dark green leaves and large, dark crimson flowers**

NAME: **VALERIAN**
VALERIANA OFFICINALIS
FAMILY: **VALERIANACEAE**

Type: Hardy perennial
USDA zone: Z9–11
Description: Valerian has shiny, round, deeply grooved, green stems and narrow, dark-green leaves that give off a scent similar to horseradish. It bears tall shoots with clusters of tiny, pale pink flowers.
Height: 2–5ft (60cm–1.5m).
How to grow: Sow seed in spring under glass in a soil-based compost. Valerian may also be propagated by division in spring.
Where to grow: Valerian enjoys a moist soil and a position in either full sun or partial shade. It makes a very good border plant, but keep well to the back because of its height.
Flowering period: The clusters of pale pink flowers appear in mid-summer.
Maintenance: Remove any flowers to encourage the growth of the rhizomes. Cut down any growth above ground in autumn.
Harvesting and uses: Lift the roots of second-year plants after the leaves have died off and use fresh or dried. Remove the pale, fibrous roots to leave the edible rhizome which can be sliced and dried. The roots are distilled for oil and liquid extracts. The oil is used in perfumes, and the extracts in flavourings for soft drinks, condiments and ice cream.
Pests and problems: Valerian is prone to attack by aphids. The scent of the roots, especially when dried, attracts cats.
Other species and varieties: Nard spike *Valeriana celtica* has brownish-yellow flowers and is grown in rock gardens.
Valeriana edulis is a North American species with a long, tapering root that is sometimes cooked as a vegetable.
Cretan spikenard *Valeriana phu* is an ornamental garden plant with white flowers.

NAME: **VERVAIN**
VERBENA OFFICINALIS
FAMILY: **VERBENACEAE**

Type: Hardy perennial
USDA zone: Z9–11
Description: Vervain has dull, greyish-green toothed leaves and a slightly hairy, branching stem. Slim spikes of tiny, pale lilac-pink flowers.
Height: 3ft (90cm).
Where to grow: The herb enjoys a well-drained, moist soil in a sunny position. It is not grown as an ornamental, but can be used as a 'filler' in the herb garden.
How to grow: Sow under cover in spring or autumn. Place seed on the surface of the soil and press well in. When large enough to handle, the seedlings should be thinned to 12in (30cm) apart. The plants can also be divided in spring and stem cuttings can be taken in summer.
Flowering period: The flowers bloom from late summer until early autumn.
Maintenance: Cut down any above-ground growth in late autumn. A general fertilizer can be given in spring.
Harvesting and uses: Harvest the green flowering plant and use fresh or dried. It has wide-ranging medical uses, and the whole plants or leaves are used to make infusions and preparations. Vervain tea can be drunk as a stimulant, relieving nervous tension and fevers.
Pests and problems: None.
Other species and varieties: Blue Vervain *Verbena hastata* is indigenous to the US and is unofficially used medicinally.
Burry Vervain *Verbena Lappulaceae* is a West Indian herb that bears pale blue flowers.

WARNING: Large doses can cause nausea. Do not take during pregnancy.

NAME: **WINTER SAVORY:** *SATUREJA MONTANA*
FAMILY: **LABIATAE**

Type: Hardy perennial

USDA zone: Z9–11

Description: Winter savory has a hairy, square, branching stem and small, pointed, dark green leaves. It bears whorls of white, pale pink or pale purple flowers.

Height: 4–16in (10–40cm).

Where to grow: Winter savory enjoys a light, sandy soil and a position in full sun. It makes a very useful edging plant.

How to grow: Seed, which is variable, should be sown in spring or autumn and the seedlings thinned to 18in (45cm) apart. Some plants will die back in winter, while others will keep their leaves. The plants can also be divided in spring or autumn, and stem cuttings taken in summer.

Flowering period: The flowers bloom in late summer and early autumn.

Maintenance: Prune in late spring. Cut back each autumn and replace every three years.

Harvesting and uses: Harvest the leaves and use fresh. They can also be dried, although this tends to make them tough. Young, green branches can be cut and frozen. The herb has a stronger, sharper flavour than summer savory *Satureja hortensis* and is excellent in stuffings and stews. It is also an important ingredient of salami and other processed meats. The leaves can be infused in vinegar and oil and added to salad dressings.

Pests and problems: None.

Other species and varieties: Creeping winter savory *Satureja spicigera* syn. *Satureja repanda* has deep green leaves and tiny, white flowers. It grows to a height of just 3in (7.5cm). Thyme-scented savory *Satureja thymbra* has oblong leaves and pink flowers.
Satureja coerula is a late flowering variety with blue flowers. It is suitable for the rock garden.

BELOW **Winter savory is a small, woody perennial with aromatic leaves and whorls of white, pale pink or pale purple flowers**

NAME: **WITCH HAZEL**
HAMAMELIS VIRGINIANA
FAMILY: **HAMAMELIDACEAE**

Type: Hardy shrub or small tree
USDA zone: Z9–11
Description: Witch hazel has oval, wavy-edged leaves that turn yellow in autumn, a gggstem of smooth, grey bark and clusters of scented, bright yellow flowers.
Height: 8–10ft (2.4–3m).
Where to grow: Witch hazel enjoys a damp, lime-free soil with plenty of humus dug in. It prefers a sunny site, or one in partial shade. It is widely grown as an ornamental herb.
How to grow: Sow the seed in autumn. Germination is both slow and erratic. It can also be propagated by softwood cuttings taken in summer, or by layering in the early autumn. Any rooted suckers can be transplanted to make new plants.
Flowering period: Clusters of flowers appear when the leaves drop off in autumn, followed by black nuts that do not often ripen until the following summer.
Maintenance: Cut out any suckers every year and cut back untidy growth after flowering.
Harvesting and uses: Gather the twigs and branches in spring and collect the leaves in summer. Witch hazel is used externally for sprains, bruises, and insect bites. It is cultivated for its value to the pharmaceutical and cosmetics industries.
Pests and problems: None.
Other species and varieties: *Hamamelis mollis* is an ornamental oriental witch hazel that flowers in winter.

WARNING: A tincture produced from the bark or leaves could disfigure the skin.

NAME: **WORMWOOD**
ARTEMISIA ABSINTHIUM
FAMILY: **COMPOSITAE**

Type: Hardy perennial
USDA zone: Z9–11
Description: Wormwood is a bitter herb with aromatic, deeply cut, grey-green leaves and spikes of small, insignificant, yellow flowers. It dies down in winter and reappears in spring.
Height: 2–3ft (60cm–1m).
Where to grow: Wormwood will grow in any soil, but it does best in a soil that is light, dry and well-drained. It prefers full sun, but it will grow in some shade. It makes an attractive border plant. If it is grown near cabbages it will deter cabbage white butterflies.
How to grow: Sow the seed in autumn as soon as it is ripe, or in spring, in shallow drills. Thin or transplant seedlings to 18in–3ft

ABOVE **Wormwood (***Artemisia absinthium***) is a sub shrub with grey-green foliage, with silky hairs on both sides**

(45cm–1m) apart. It can also be propagated by root division in spring, or by taking semi-hardwood cuttings in late summer.

Flowering period: Flowers appear in summer.

Maintenance: Cut back to 1–2in (2.5–5cm) above the crown in autumn. Wormwood can be invasive and must be kept under control.

Harvesting and uses: Cut and dry the leaves and tops in late summer. Dried stems are good in flower arrangements, and dried leaves can be used in mixtures to ward off moths. The herb is used commercially to make vermouth and other aperitifs.

Pests and problems: None.

Other species and varieties: Roman wormwood *Artemisia pontica* has very aromatic, feathery, silver foliage and a spreading rootstalk.

Sweet wormwood *Artemisia annua* is a giant annual, with bright green, saw-toothed leaves. It is fast-growing and can reach a height of 4–6ft (1.5–3m).

Artemisia ludoviciana 'Silver Queen' is a cultivar with willow-like, jagged, silver leaves that bears plumes of yellow-grey flowers.

WARNING. Do not plant wormwood next to culinary or medicinal herbs such as caraway or sage. The rain washes a growth-inhibiting toxin out of its leaves that will affect nearby plants.

NAME: YARROW
ACHILLEA MILLEFOLIUM
FAMILY: COMPOSITAE

Type: Hardy perennial
USDA zone: Z9–11
Description: Yarrow has a sturdy, upright, furrowed stem with long, feathery, grey-green foliage and dense, flat-topped heads of whitish, pink or lilac flowers. The flowers attract many beneficial insects including ladybirds and parasitic wasps.

Height: Up to 24in (60cm).

Where to grow: Yarrow prefers a moderately rich, well-drained soil in full sun. It can be planted as a lawn. If it is to be cultivated in the herb border, it should be segregated from other plants because it is so invasive. It is not suitable for growing indoors.

How to grow: Sow the seed in a light compost in late spring and place in an unheated propagator. The plants should be 6in (15cm) apart for a lawn and 12in (30cm) apart for a border. It can also be propagated by division of the readily-spreading roots in spring.

Flowering period: The flowers bloom between summer and late autumn.

Maintenance: Dead-head to produce a second crop of flowers.

Harvesting and uses: Harvest the plants when they are in flower and dry them for use in infusions, liquid extracts and lotions.

Pests and problems: Variants do not come true from seed. Mildew can be a problem during hot summers.

Other species and varieties: *Achillea millefolium* 'Cerise Queen' is a cultivar that produces deep pink flowers in mid-summer, and is less invasive than the species.

Achillea millefolium 'Lilac Beauty' is another cultivar that is less invasive than the species, and produces lilac-pink flowers in mid-summer. Musk yarrow *Achillea moschata* has ferny leaves and white flowers. It grows to a height of 8in (20cm).

WARNING: Continued use of yarrow can make skin light-sensitive.

Glossary of gardening terms

ACID A term applied to soil that has a pH value of less than 7. Acid soil is deficient in lime and contains few basic minerals.

ALKALINE With a pH value of more than 7. Soil derived from chalk or limestone is usually alkaline and has a pH reading of more than 7. Most herbs will thrive in alkaline soil.

ANNUAL A plant that is grown from seed, which germinates, flowers, seeds and dies within one growing season.

ANTHER The part of the stamen that contains the pollen.

BIENNIAL A plant that completes its life-cycle in two years. It produces stems and leaves during the first year, flowers in the second, then sets seed and dies.

BRACT A small modified leaf, often protective, at the base of a flower.

BROADCAST Scatter seed evenly over an area of ground rather than sowing in drills.

BULB An underground stem consiting of fleshy scales that store food for the embryo plant.

COLD FRAME An unheated structure used to protect plants in winter. It is usually made from bricks, with a glass or plastic cover.

COMPOST
1 A growing medium containing ingredients such as peat, loam, sand and leaf mould, in which seeds are sown and plants potted.
2 Recycled, decomposed plant material and other organic matter used as a soil improver and as a mulch.

CROCKS Broken pieces of clay pot placed in the bottom of a container. Their purpose is to improve drainage and provide air circulation to the root system of the plants.

CROWN The basal part of a herbaceous perennial, at or just below the surface of the soil, from which the roots and shoots grow.

CULTIVAR A variety of plant that has been cultivated, rather than one that grows naturally in the wild.

CUTTING A piece of stem, root, shoot, bud or leaf cut from the parent plant to be used to grow more specimens of that plant.

DEAD HEAD Remove spent flowers or flower heads to encourage further growth, another flowering, and to prevent self-seeding.

DECIDUOUS Plants, especially trees and shrubs, that lose their leaves at the end of the growing season. The leaves of the plant are then renewed at the start of the next growing season.

DIVISION Increasing plants by dividing dormant roots into two or more parts.

DORMANCY The resting period of a seed or plant when there is a temporary slowing or cessation of growth, usually in winter.

DOUBLE DIGGING Term used when soil is dug to the depth of two spades.

DRILL A straight furrow made in the soil for sowing seed in a line.

EVERGREEN Plants, mostly shrubs and trees, that keep most of their leaves all year round, although some of the older leaves are lost regularly throughout the year. They provide structure in the garden during the winter.

GERMINATION The changes that take place as a seed starts to grow and the root and shoot emerge.

GROUND COVER Low-growing plants that cover the ground quickly and are good for suppressing weeds.

HABIT The characteristic shape and general appearance of a plant.

HALF-HARDY Plants that will over-winter successfully outdoors in a sheltered position. They may not survive severe frosts.

HARDENING OFF Process of acclimatizing young plants to outside temperatures. Plants are placed outside for increasing lengths of time during the day and put back under cover at night. This can take two or three weeks.

HARDY Plants that are able to survive the winter outdoors, including frosty conditions, without protection.

HERBACEOUS Term for plants with non-woody stems that die down at the end of each growing season.

HUMUS Crumbly, dark brown, decayed vegetable matter formed by the partial breakdown of plant remains by bacteria. An example is well-made garden compost.

HYBRID A plant that has been created from parents of different species or genera.

INFUSION A liquid obtained by steeping herbs in boiling water.

INVASIVE Vigorous-growing plant that will suffocate neighbouring plants if it is not controlled or grown in a container.

LANCEOLATE Shaped like a narrow spear and tapering at each end. Usually used to describe the shape of a leaf.

LAYERING Method of propagation in which a stem is pegged down into the soil and encouraged to root while still attached to the parent plant.

LIME Compounds of calcium. The proportion of lime in a soil determines whether it is acid, neutral or alkaline. Some soils have a predominant lime content.

LOAM Soil composed of an even mixture of clay and sand and a balance of nutrients. Loam is well-drained, fertile and retains moisture well.

MULCH A layer of material applied to the surface of the soil surface to improve its structure, conserve moisture, protect plant roots from frost, and suppress weeds.

NODE The point on a stem from which leaves, shoots, branches or flowers arise.

NUTRIENTS Minerals used to develop proteins and other compounds necessary for the growth and well-being of a plant.

OVATE Egg-shaped, broader at the base, and more pointed at the tip. Usually used to describe leaves.

PEAT Partly-decayed organic matter with a water-retaining structure. Usually acid, it is used in growing composts or mulches. For environmental reasons, peat substitutes such as coconut fibre are often used.

PERENNIAL A plant, usually herbaceous, that lives for at least three seasons. It flowers every year, dies down in winter, and new shoots appear each spring. Woody-based perennials die down only partially.

pH A scale used to indicate the alkalinity or acidity of the soil, which ranges from 1–14. A pH reading of 7 is neutral; below pH 7 is acid soil, and more than pH 7 is alkaline.

PINCHING OUT The removal of the growing tips of a plant, using the finger and thumb, to encourage the production of side-shoots. It is also known as 'stopping'.

PINNATE Pairs of leaflets arranged on either side of a stem, usually opposite each other.

PRICK OUT Transfer seedlings from the bed or container in which they germinated to pots or areas of the garden where they will have room to develop and grow.

PROPAGATION Increasing plants vegetatively or by seed.

PROSTRATE Growing low or flat over the surface of the ground.

RACEME Short lateral stalk springing from a central stem to which are attached clusters of separate flowers.

RHIZOME A branched underground stem that bears roots and shoots.

RUNNER A slender, horizontally spreading stem that runs along the surface of the soil, rooting at intervals.

SELF-SEEDING Term applied to plants that shed their seeds around them after flowering, from which new plants will grow the following year.

SPECIES Plants of a specific type and constant character that breed together. Seed-grown species are consistently true to type.

TAP ROOT The long, strong main root of a plant that grows downwards into the soil.

TENDER Term for plants that are susceptible to damage at low temperatures and cannot survive outside during winter, They should be brought indoors before the first frosts.

TILTH Soil that has been broken down into small crumbs by correct digging and raking. It is an ideal, fine, crumbly, top layer.

TOPIARY The art of clipping and training dense-leaved shrubs and trees into geometric and unusual shapes.

TOPSOIL The fertile, uppermost layer of soil.

TRIFOLIATE Consisting of three leaflets.

UMBEL A flat-topped or rounded flower cluster on individual flower stalks radiating from a central point.

VARIEGATED Leaves or flowers that exhibit more than one colour. Generally describes leaves with white or cream markings.

VARIETY Variant of an original species or hybrid, often used to describe variants induced by cultivation (cultivars).

WHORL Three or more leaves or flowers forming a ring at one stem joint.

About the author

Yvonne Cuthbertson discovered the joys of herb gardening some years ago when she and her family moved into a non-working farm. It came complete with two acres of uncultivated farmland where she set about making a large herb gaden. This was just the start of her fascination with herbs and, as the years progressed, more house moves enabled her to make several more such gardens.

A former primary school head teacher, Yvonne holds a Royal Horticultural Society General Certificate in Horticulture. She has written for a variety of publications both in Britain and other parts of the world, on topics including gardening, herbalism, antiques, conservation and alternative medicine. She often combines her love of writing with a passion for photography.

Yvonne and her husband recently moved to a newly-renovated home in Somerset. She has already started the process of creating another herb garden.

Index

References to illustrations of herbs are in **bold**.
Where there is more than one page number main references are shown by *italics*.

GMC Publications
Castle Place, 166 High Street, Lewes, East Sussex BN7 1XU, United Kingdom
Tel: 01273 488005   Fax: 01273 402866
E-mail: pubs@thegmcgroup.com   Website: www.gmcbooks.com

Contact us for a complete catalogue, or visit our website. Orders by credit card are accepted.